CHURCH
BUILDINGS

A STRATEGIC GUIDE TO DESIGN, RENOVATION, AND CONSTRUCTION

KATIE BURCH

LUCIDBOOKS

Church Buildings:
A Strategic Guide to Design, Renovation, and Construction
Copyright © 2016 by Katie Burch
Icons on cover and throughout text by Jonathan Rollins

Published by Lucid Books in Houston, TX.
www.LucidBooks.net

ISBN 10: 1-63296-094-X
ISBN 13: 978-1-63296-094-8
eISBN 10: 1-63296-095-8
eISBN 13: 978-1-63296-095-5

Special Sales: Most Lucid Books titles are available in special quantity discounts. Custom imprinting or excerpting can also be done to fit special needs. Contact Lucid Books at info@lucidbooks.net.

TABLE OF CONTENTS

ACKNOWLEDGMENTS

Joyful, heartfelt thanks to these contributors, encouragers, and inspirers:

Ken, Grady, and Jackson Burch, Justin Hyde, Jared Polak, Mike and Rhonda Collier, Laura Portner, Danielle Walker, Ted and Mary Walker, Peter Morissette, and the PLANNorth Team: Darcee, Mandi, Sam, Marissa, Kim, Jenn, and Lacey

INTRODUCTION

When your church first started out, life in ministry was probably very different. As you worked to help the church grow, you may have thought, "If our church were just giving $500 each week, we could do so much," or, "If we could reach 50 members, we would feel stable." But now, maybe you have 300 people, and your giving is higher than ever. What many people don't realize is that when leaders are growing an organization, such as a church or a business, what may have seemed as if it would be a total success can bring significant burdens when it actually arrives. The weight of needing to care for 300 people, when you started with three, is a feeling much the same as growing any business or venture. The joy and burden of growth walk hand in hand, and most days it can feel more like a rollercoaster ride than a walk.

Growth carries immense joy and satisfaction, but uncertainty can cling to every step. Having felt this pressure when starting our architectural company, I have always felt an understanding for pastors as they manage the growth of their church. When my business was just starting out, I was incredibly excited to be working with a team of people passionate to help churches create the perfect building, but also felt overwhelmed as to how I would get the tools they needed, how I would nurture my team, and how we would fund our growing needs.

The more I considered it, the more I realized we needed to find a way to start sharing the right information—at the most critical times—to those who would benefit most from the knowledge. As we worked to better share the right information, we clarified the two major areas where churches needed our company. Most churches need two things when growing their church's facilities:

1. Reliable information at every stage of growth in order to facilitate solid decisions
2. Someone to fully design the spaces where their vision would grow

The latter was very specific and required major resources in order to create a physical representation of another person's vision. But the first existed in our heads, available to anyone who asked and no one who didn't. Church leaders who could ask a church planning expert for advice had the major edge, and those who were scrambling to piece together advice from the internet were at a loss. Ironically, one of the critical times that churches most need reliable information is in the beginning stages of planning. So, we started offering small, inexpensive, focused services for churches. With these planning services available, churches could reach out to us if they needed guidance about choosing the right site, long-term planning, or simply clarifying their church's vision.

Share what you know would become the most important core value of our company and the chief motivation for our book. *Church Buildings* is meant to organize the most important pieces of knowledge a church needs to know about facility growth. This book is meant to share what we know.

A Note about the Resources in This Book

We have provided the following items to help you throughout the book:

Rules of thumb: The sections will give you figures and specific information to help you in church planning. (See sections with the 👍 icon.)

Questions to ponder: Critical questions for you to think through are set apart on the page. (See sections with the ❓ icon.)

Free resources: Throughout the book, we have provided links to additional documents that will help you as you work through the planning, design, and construction stages.

Glossary: These definitions will help you fully participate in critical discussions with your architect, contractor, and leadership teams. Glossary terms have also been bolded throughout the text.

Chapter 1

CASTING YOUR VISION

S ooner or later in the life of every church, physical space for worship and ministry becomes a "thing." Some leaders are thinking of growth and eyeing land for sale before they have their first ten members. Others begin considering growth only when there are no chairs left in the sanctuary. Most fall somewhere in between. The truth is that by the time the sanctuary is crowded, there's an urgency involved that can cloud the judgment of even the most levelheaded pastors and elders, and for good reason. Losing a potential member of the church family due to lack of physical space should not be a state that any church reaches.

Instead, churches can work to be proactive. At every phase of growth, church leadership can pave the way for an organized, healthy facility growth plan, starting with their vision for the church. This chapter will help you think through your vision for the growth of your church's facilities. Clarifying your vision will allow you to articulate how that vision will translate to the physical surroundings and spaces—in short, casting your vision for the future of the church in a way that everyone clearly understands and commits to.

STARTING WITH THE VISION

Defining the vision is the crucial first step every church must start with. Your church must know its core values, its goals, and where it's going before determining what kind of building will fulfill those needs. The vision will govern every decision you make and will save you both time and money.

Tackling a huge project like church building planning can feel overwhelming. When looking at an undertaking like this, the question people usually ask is, "Where do I begin?" Often, people wrongly assume that the first item to discuss is the floor plan. This assumption is a significant misconception. The floor plan, like any other piece of this giant puzzle, is only a tool. Many decisions have to be made before moving to the stage of floor plans. At times, I meet with a church leader or pastor and learn they have a floor plan sketched and "ready for drafting." However, to draw a floor plan prior to an in-depth conversation about the mission of the church is putting the cart far before the horse.

In the first architectural firm I worked with, the office had a golden rule: "Only draw something if you are 100% sure what it is and how it works." What this rule meant was that employees should never draw lines on details, sections, and plans without knowing what materials were involved, because major construction problems could occur. Over the years, I have seen the significance of this rule and how many setbacks and failures it prevents. Today, one of our firm's rules is, "We don't draw before we know the vision of the church." We have to know what the pastor's game plan is, how many people are on board with the vision, who the key players are, and what ministries they head up.

Your primary objective and first task should be to answer these types of questions: Where are we going? Where do we want to be 20 years from now? Will this church grow to 400 people and then plant another church? Or, do we want to grow this community's first 500-person congregation? Most pastors can answer these questions. Next, think of what that situation might look like physically if those goals were to be accomplished. In order to achieve that vision, what should you do today? What I have just described is the basic thinking behind

master planning*. Master planning will create a long-term outline for a series of projects for a church. When completed, a master plan should accommodate the growth and full ministry potential of the church. Such an exercise is meant to offer guidance and vision—as opposed to rigidity—to the various groups who will implement the differing phases of the development.

While considering your master plan, keep this in mind: the best-laid plans will change. Your plan is going to evolve. You will spend countless hours articulating your visions, and your architect will finally put pen to paper on a scheme you love. But you won't draw up a master plan and then eventually build that exact master plan. You will instead draw a master plan to create a framework and cast your vision, and then you will adapt it with each new step. Seven years later, when you're in phase three of your growth and looking back at the original master plan, you will see differences. Sometimes, people think, "We already master planned, and we have to stick to that exact plan." To adopt this mindset is shortsighted, though, because drawings are just tools. Master planning is a thoughtful, educated, vision-casting exercise, with the understanding that the translation of that vision will certainly change over time.

Note: *At our company, PlanNorth, we make it a point to keep editable files of each version of a church's master planning exercises on file for easy modifications as the phases develop over the years. You can certainly ask your team to do the same, and keep the files for your reference. This avoids redundancy in time and effort, and helps to align your team over time.*

While you are considering the long-term facility needs of the church, now is also the time to re-evaluate your ministry vision.

---

* **Master plan**—a long-term outline for a series of projects for a church which, when completed, accomplish the appropriate facilities for growth and full ministry potential of the church. A master plan is meant to offer guidance and vision, as opposed to rigidity, to the various groups who will implement the different phases of the development.

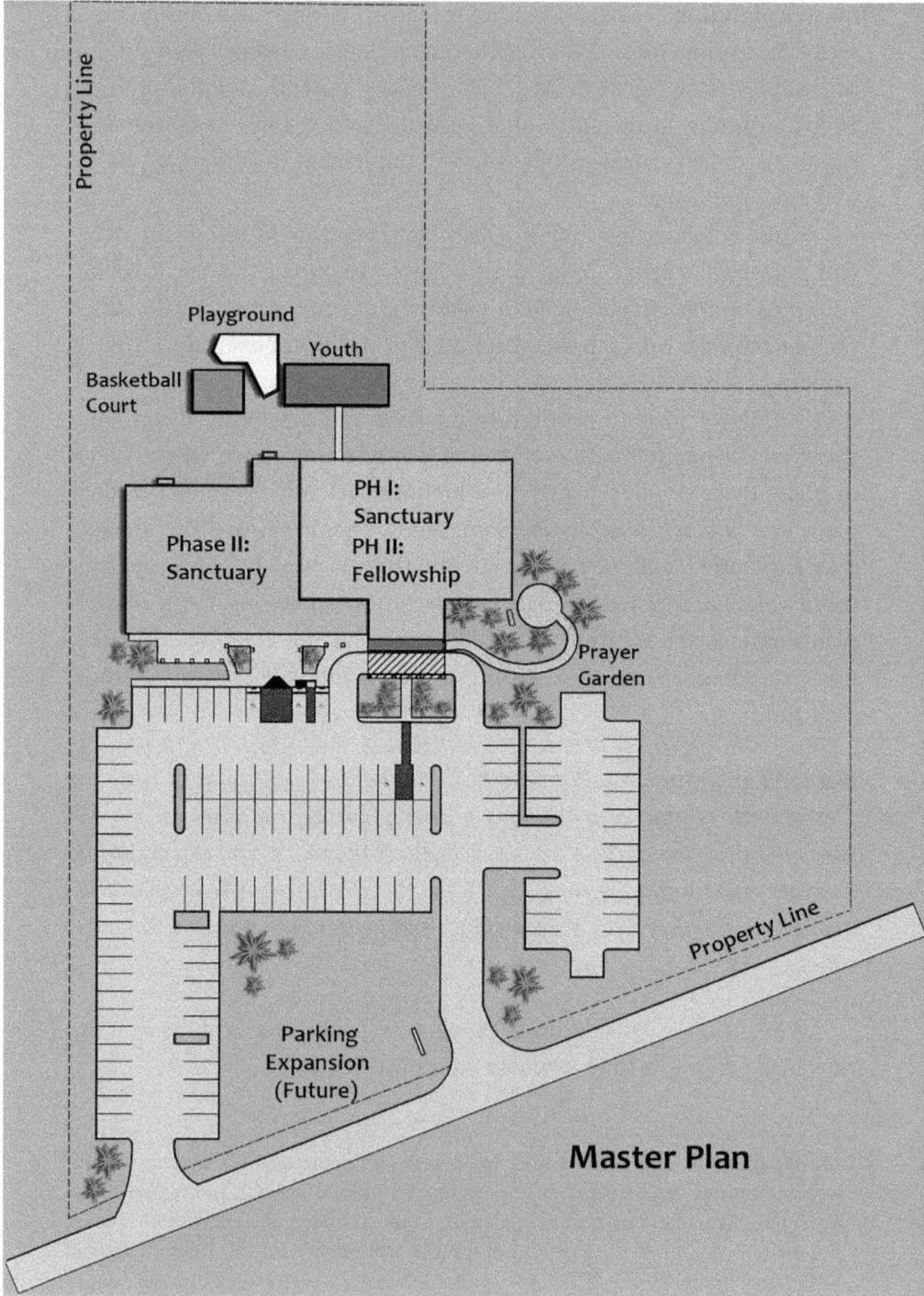

Master Plan

> **While you are considering the long-term facility needs of the church, now is also the time to re-evaluate your ministry vision.**

So what does this mean in terms of practical steps? How do you define your own vision for the church? Let's explore what the word "vision" means and implies.

The type of vision we are discussing is not so much experiential as it is strategic. Vision anticipates and acts in preparation for what is to come. Vision is at once creative and yet informed, vivid and sober at the same time. To create a vision in the early stages (or to push yourself to understand your vision better, or to re-evaluate your ministry vision), you will have to put details aside for a season, in search of a strong, big-picture definition.

If you are not by nature "visionary," and even if you are, a list of thought-provoking questions can help you define exactly what the vision for your church may be. Once you are able to articulate these thoughts to others (even if it means just reading it from a list you've compiled!), you are in a much better place to make decisions about the facilities which would best serve your church.

Visit www.churchbuildingguide.com for a copy of our Vision Plan Outline, designed to help churches define their individual visions.

(?) Where do most of your resources go?

One telling question is, where do most of your resources go? Many churches cite missions as one of their top priorities. If that's true, as an architect, I should be able to draw certain conclusions from that. For example, a church who gives sacrificially to missions of any type is highly unlikely to be interested in high-end finishes and elaborately designed buildings. Now, do remember that human beings are involved. People, and architects, can get swept away in the moment of trying to design a beautiful building. You would be hard-pressed to find a church who truly desires an ugly facility (I know of only one). What it will come down to is priorities. As building planning and design develop, needs begin to grow and costs inevitably go up. When there is an issue, think about the vision of the church. Which solution best fulfills the overall vision? In 90% of the cases you encounter, answering this question solves your problem and provides you with the clarification you need. It is vitally important that your vision for the church facilities are aligned with your vision for the actual church.

> (?) **Which solution best fulfills the overall vision?**

As you are defining your vision (for both the facilities and the church), consider having a conversation with your architect. Architects by their very nature are not only detail-oriented, but visionaries. But in order for them to apply that skill of vision, they have to know your purpose for the church. Their talent is to create how your facilities can best work for your purposes, and their visionary abilities make it possible for them to conceptualize exactly how your purpose would translate into reality. Ultimately, they will solve the puzzle between your needs, your budget, and all the idiosyncrasies which make up construction and design.

WHAT WILL YOUR BUILDING LOOK LIKE?

How will your facility look once it is built? Well, it can look however you want it to. What you first need to identify is the driving factor for this decision. By now, you can probably guess that your vision will be the driver. But what does that mean in practical application, and how does it translate into concrete decisions?

The key to determining the look of the church is to first decide how you want people to **feel**. One of the first things we ask our customers to do is think for a bit and then tell us the four words that describe how they want their church to feel in their space. It is then our job to use the built environment to accomplish those goals. Here are some of our most common customer goals:

- "We want them to feel welcome."
- "We want them to feel comfortable."
- "We want them to know we are young and growing."
- "We want them to feel safe."
- "We want them to feel the diversity."
- "We want them to know Jesus here."
- "We want them to feel loved and cared for."

These are some of the examples we hear from churches. Once our company learns the church's defining words, we post the words in our studio near the rest of the project's inspiration. Those words are the drivers for every decision we make about aesthetics. Research tells us what types of colors and materials yield feelings—by pairing this research with a church's general preferences, we are able to create a trusted, authentic recipe for design decisions. You can implement a similar process.

The key to determining the look of the church is to first decide how you want people to *feel*.

Most people are familiar with the idea that first impressions are imprinted into the human brain in a matter of seconds, and the importance of setting a good initial impression is highly important in many contexts. However, because churches are ministering to the social, spiritual, and physical needs of people, first impressions work a little different in church buildings. People are much more likely to spend time in a church that's aesthetically unappealing than in a store or a restaurant that's questionable. Could a church operate in less than clean, less than attractive, and less than adequate facilities for decades, yet continue to grow? Yes. They can, and they do. The question becomes one of culture.

Humans by nature subconsciously draw information from their surroundings—this is why there are so many research studies done on first impressions, sales presentations, interviewing, and other similar areas. So when people come into your space and see simple, clean walls, bare concrete floors, and neatly organized bulletin boards, you don't need a sign that says, "We do not believe in spending money on superficial luxuries." People can tell. Alternatively, if you enter a church lobby featuring a '90s mauve and hunter green color scheme and bulletin boards showing nothing but historical photos, one might draw the conclusion that history (i.e. the past) is the focus. It's just human nature. So, here is a question to ask your church staff: is your current building space delivering the correct message about your culture?

In this way, you put your focus on setting the parameters and the framework for the vision. One scenario might be that you're in the middle of a high density area, and you are not visible from the freeway. Maybe you simply need to be seen so that people know your church body is there! In that case, maybe one of your words could be "presence." Across the board, the design team would work to integrate the building into its surroundings by doing things like providing sidewalk lighting leading from nearby establishments, or adding greenspace, parklets, and shared benches connecting the church to the neighbors. Then, on the top of the church and visible from the freeway, they could design a tiny neon cross so that every driver on the freeway knows, "Hey, inside there— there's a church." The word is presence, and just that word is enough visionary framework for an architect to conceptualize how to make the built environment perform in that way.

One of our projects was built on a park that included an amphitheater and various amenities. The church wanted to relate to that park—they wanted the inside of their church to have an indoor-outdoor feel, which can be challenging in Texas. It was important to them, though, that patrons of the park could see what was going on at the church, and vice versa. To accomplish their goal, we designed big porches with shade and privacy walls, and indoor spaces with strategically framed views.

Is your current building space delivering the correct message about your culture?

Understand that you have many, many creative options to accomplish your goals and to make people feel a certain way. Often, it's easy to think that in order to achieve a specific goal, you will have to spend x amount of dollars and use a particular design, but you usually have multiple avenues that will bring you to the same result. Early on in my business, I was working on a low-budget sanctuary renovation with a church. One of the women in charge of the project had visited a church in Dallas that had an enormous, beautiful lobby featuring a glass mosaic tile wall and a massive, 30-foot cross suspended from the ceiling. The cross was reflective and cast a striking shadow, and everybody felt wonderful when walking into the space.

The woman showed me pictures of this lobby several times. But I am a realist, albeit a very positive one, so I broke the news to her gently that it wasn't in the cards. Their church is in a very low-income area, and they had very little money (they often struggled to pay their light bill). She was noticeably disappointed. So, I decided to dwell on how to get a glass mosaic wall with a 30-foot cross into their church. I mentioned the situation to an older architect who had come into my office one day for a meeting. He laughed out loud and said, "You're going to learn that people who show you pictures aren't asking for a copy of what they see. They want you to make them feel the same way they do when they see the picture."

So, I did what many architects do when they feel like throwing their hands up. I decided to walk around a hardware store and see what the cheapest materials actually were. As a result of my field trip, I learned that bare metal panels are cheap and very reflective. I also came to appreciate the rough planks of wood residing in the bargain section. After a trip to the store for LED rope lights, we were ready to roll. We designed a 12-foot-tall version of the showpiece in the inspiration picture and installed it behind the baptistery, in their very old building in the roughest area of town. The day I showed up to check on the construction of our little masterpiece, the woman met me in tears. She couldn't believe we had somehow copied the picture. To her, the mission was accomplished because she had the same feeling in her building as she did in the church in Dallas.

Aesthetics as they relate to churches are only important in that they support the bigger vision. Vision will determine color and material choices, ceilings, roofs, floor plans, and everything else. The vision tells us where to put pockets of stone, fabric, or tile for acoustic purposes, or durability, or for creating places of solitude—all of these choices are important because they are pieces of a bigger puzzle coming together.

> **Aesthetics as they relate to churches are only important in that they support the bigger vision.**

So what words do you want to accomplish? Your job is to make that decision and then set your architect in motion. Let your architect come back with their best efforts to design a space that aligns with your words, and then ask your questions out loud, "Do I feel welcome? Do I feel safe? Do I feel loved and cared for?"

> **How do you want your facilities to be used, specifically?**

Now that the juices are flowing with ideas for how you want your church to feel, I want to open the conversation of how your church building is going to work as the ministry tool it should be. How do you want your facilities to be used, specifically? Here are some of my favorite conversations about maxing out your building to support your vision for the church.

THE THIRD PLACE

The **third place** is the idea that a place other than your house and your workplace functions as an integral part of your life. It is a special location that becomes a key part of your world. Perhaps a coffee shop or a library is a person's third place, especially if they don't have internet access or an extra space to work at home. Sometimes a third place exists for a person for a limited time, and other times for a lifetime. At one point, your place could have been your grandma's house, or your friend's backyard.

What if the church building could become a third place for your church members?

A couple of years ago, one of the men who worked for our company went to lunch every day for about 45 minutes. I knew his family lived pretty far out in the country, and after asking him one day where he went, I found out he went to his church. He simply grabbed his lunch and went to his church to eat. This was a foreign concept to me at the time, and I found it so interesting that he felt welcome enough to go there every day. The church had tables set up, and he ate with whoever was there, or with no one. That was it. The church had provided a place of peace and rest as a blessing to its congregation. Some churches take their vision even further than this and have food prepared daily on a "pay as you can" basis.

Many people are not naturally geared toward sharing their personal lives with strangers. We have to recognize, though, that if people were to have lunch with the same group every day, it is much more likely that they would get to know each other in a more meaningful way. Let's say people are together in a common area on a regular basis because they feel relaxed and have free water and Wi-Fi. In six months, how would relationships be different among that group?

So, with respect to buildings, the concept of the church as a third place is simply to meet people where they are by fulfilling needs that are not met elsewhere. Sometimes "meet them where they're at" means simply providing a place to sit down and have lunch in a peaceful, comfortable environment away from the workplace.

MULTIPURPOSE SPACES: MORE THAN A CATCHPHRASE

One of the challenges church leaders face is that, at times, they have become so accustomed to the general approach, "We'll make it work." The idea of not stacking chairs for one week, or even of owning chairs at all, is such a stretch that they sometimes have difficulty seeing past that.

As you head into the church planning season, however, you will need to reframe the "make it work" approach and think carefully about your strategy for multi-purpose buildings. Here's the deal: as church leaders transition into new spaces, they often assume that the spaces themselves don't matter because they will simply work with whatever setup they get. Even more commonly, church leaders are often geared to think, "Let's use every square inch of the building, every day." That is great in theory. However, a better goal would be to offer people what they need every day. Sometimes, people need quiet, and sometimes they need dynamic energy. Where in your building would they go for those needs?

Energy created in different types of spaces is contagious.

On a basic level, churches should have different types of spaces. Even if these spaces are multipurpose—in fact, especially if the spaces are multipurpose—people need both quiet spaces and loud spaces, spaces generally reserved for prayer or counseling conversations, reverent spaces for contemplation, and spaces for activity and music. Energy created in different types of spaces is contagious. This energy yields a rich environment for ministries to play off one another's successes, participate in each other's journeys, and learn organically through others.

As leaders are discussing the multipurpose concept with my team, metal buildings often come up. Actually, they are the #1 request of churches with the "make it work" approach. These buildings are very functional, lend themselves to great flexibility, and are economical to boot. The very nature of the open spaces, high ceilings, and open feel appeal to almost everyone in the church community. However, from a building perspective, what leaders often aren't thinking about is this: that building they're visualizing as "open" is really only going to be open in two key areas: the sanctuary, and the foyer/lobby. Restrooms need walls, as do kitchens, classrooms, offices, break rooms, meeting rooms, conference rooms, and pretty much every other type of room. So go ahead and embrace this open concept, but do not trick yourself into thinking it will function as "multipurpose" with no design. What will happen in that scenario is a loud, uncomfortable clashing of ideas and motives, leading to ministries jockeying for position and a lack of security for children and families. If you hear nothing else in this book, understand this: *the multipurpose concept is the best concept, but there is no other concept that takes more work to get it to function well.*

Do each of your ministries feel special, and are they able to reach their full potential using the facilities they have access to? There is a huge difference between building a giant barn and telling everyone to use it how they want to, versus taking the approach of painstakingly recording the needs and wishes of each important ministry and working diligently to meet everyone's needs. Does every person in the church get everything they want for their ministry? Of course not—however, can you make sure everyone's needs are met for growth? With strategic planning and thorough research of each ministry's needs, you absolutely can.

> **Do each of your ministries feel special, and are they able to reach their full potential using the facilities they have access to?**

So what does this look like? Here's an example.

Perhaps the church needs a multimedia room with projectors or flat-screen TVs, and they need many receptacles so that people can simply set their things down and go to work (e.g., meetings and group discussions). And let's say that such a room will serve many ministries. Perhaps your church also wants a library with comfortable furniture and quiet spaces for reading and research. The church might assume they can't afford those types of luxuries. But what if the meeting room were also a library with moveable shelves, which could easily be rearranged to create separation walls accommodating multiple groups? Chances are that pastoral research will *not* take place during Sunday School time when most meetings occur. So that room can work double overtime!

A key step in multifunctional planning is simply being willing to accept that church spaces are changing, and they don't have to be how they always have been. The most important consideration to remember is how you want your people to *feel* in those spaces—think back to your four words. Are you from the school where "private" means four walls where no one can hear? Well, private also can just mean alone.

Outdoor spaces where people are not in earshot are also very private. In fact, people tend to feel less trapped and more open to discussion outdoors. Even in Texas, simple outdoor spaces with shade and a fan have become comfortable places for conversations and lunch, not to mention counseling.

Also, people need quieter spaces—spaces to pray, write, work, or just think. There's an energy in these spaces that fosters prayer and meditation, an energy that people feed off of and can feel. Even dedicating a large closet with a chair and small desk, with writing materials and Bibles, can greatly minister to church members. What if this were a space made public during the week? This is similar to the concept of a chapel, with less formality and more individuality.

We also see many fellowship areas that are not only eating spaces, but are used for athletics, receptions, and youth rallies. Sometimes, worship happens there too. On a very tight budget, this approach makes sense because the noise level is similar in all of these circumstances. You can make these types of spaces truly functional for different events by considering items like dimmable lighting (which can change a room from a sanctuary to a basketball court with the flip of a switch) and by paying special attention to sound and storage.

Remember that just because a room is multipurpose doesn't necessarily mean your church will need to take down and put up furniture constantly. Rather, it means that the room is set up for a specific type of use, and you have many tasks that need that type of use. Yes, there will be some stacking of chairs, but if you carefully plan shared usage, you can limit the takedown and pickup scenario to special occasions and still use your building at capacity.

FORM OVER FUNCTION, OR FUNCTION OVER FORM? DO I CARE?

Which is more important? Should we prioritize how well a space works or its aesthetic value? Are they related?

There's been an ongoing conversation in the architectural community about "form over function" or "function over form." Which is more important? Should we prioritize how well a space works or its aesthetic value? Are they related?

Some architects in the "purist" camp will spend real time detailing how light will fall on a floor, and the results truly are beautiful. People like this are more inclined to focus on form. On the opposite end, some are purely concerned with function. These people might say, "I can crank this out on a piece of graph paper, and you can build it tomorrow." Both camps, however, are misguided.

What both of these mindsets lose is not so much aesthetic value or the ability to use the building, but more of the *intrinsic* capabilities of the space. When you're so heavily driven by function, you can easily lose sight of the actual functionality of the church. For example, I have often heard people insist that toilets back up to one another to save on the cost of plumbing pipe. This is of course an ideal scenario, but if the building works out such that the restroom door would have to swing straight into the sanctuary, or that people could see straight into the restroom when the door was opened, then following such a "rule" lacks common sense at that point. We have to think more about the forest and less about the trees.

Equally divergent is the scenario where we become obsessed with the aesthetics of the building. Some might say, "We want a big metal building with a stone wainscot—that's all we care about." Or there's the architect who has chained himself to a certain type of window, convincing himself that the building needs will have to work around that window because it looks good.

I would encourage you to think outside these types of boxes. When you first begin planning the building that will truly meet your needs, you have no idea what it should look like. You have to first address the vision of how the building will meet your congregation's needs.

If you are making any decision based solely on looks or on preexisting ideas you had about the aesthetics, take a closer look. Are you wanting to use white limestone? Great, but first ask yourself if the limestone speaks to the overall vision. Perhaps the vision requires the building to relate to its surroundings (such as in the case of a neighborhood church), establish itself as a special place among a sea of noise (such as a church off the highway), serve as a gateway for help (such as a church in an inner-city ward), or a host of other things more important than what material goes on the building. If limestone fits in the vision context, go for it. But think about the vision first.

> When you first begin planning the building that will truly meet your needs, you have no idea what it should look like. You have to first address the vision of how the building will meet your congregation's needs.

The truth is that form and function are equally important. In tandem, they support your ministries and your vision. Corridors, foyers, and hallways are a good example. A strictly "functional" mindset might say something like this: "We're going to have as few hallways as we can manage. When we do have them, they should be small so we don't waste square footage." Here's the translation: "We will use hallways for one thing only: getting people to leave." Oops. That's not what you meant, right? An eight-foot-wide hall can be a place for a conversation and still allow space for passersby. A four-foot-wide hall is just a four-foot-wide walkway. Would you rather use 300 square feet than waste 150? A generous hall in a smaller church can also accommodate a children's check-in table, a food spread, or a set of chairs for an older couple to sit down and relax.

All of these details are functional, but they are being approached in an open-minded and informed manner. All of these details are also beautiful because they are considering how the building will affect the people in it (aesthetically, spiritually, or otherwise). Thoughtfulness, cleanliness, and kindness all influence the experiences people have when using your buildings. If you can begin to think in terms of every piece of the puzzle being both functional and beautiful, then you can begin to describe what *intrinsic* qualities you desire for your church spaces.

Action Items:

1. Create your Vision Plan. Use our form at www.churchbuildingguide.com to get started.

2. Meet with the leaders of your ministries and ask them what they need from the future church building. *Tell them you are at the very beginning phases of researching, and by no means are you making promises! You just want to listen so you can meet their needs as best as you can. What is going well, what are the pain points, and how are the facilities currently serving them?* Be sure to take notes or record the information so that it is not located only in your own head. The information must also be deliverable to others after these meetings but does not have to be typed neatly on letterhead—the point is to be able to share the information. Key ministries, such as the children's or women's/men's ministries, could be larger conversations with a group.

   Once you have spoken with everyone, you can begin to prioritize the needs. Resist the urge to turn this exercise into a floor plan. Just consider which ministries might reasonably share spaces. In this process, you will need to flesh some information out. For example, some ministries require dedicated space, while some ministries wish they did, but actually do not.

3. Write down your recent average attendances, and any events that spurred large crowds.

   If you can physically see activities on an actual calendar, you can begin to visualize the framework of what will happen inside your building from day to day. If you already have a building and are bursting at the seams, be careful to tag important ministries that are severely underserved space-wise so that your team can discuss these ministries further.

Visit www.churchbuildingguide.com for a sample scheduling tool.

Discussion Topics:

1. What are the top 5 words you would use to describe your church's culture?

    a. _____

    b. _____

    c. _____

    d. _____

    e. _____

2. What are some words that describe how you want your church to feel?

    a. _____

    b. _____

    c. _____

    d. _____

3. Do you know if each of your ministries feels special? What value do those ministries bring the church as a whole? Think through some examples of how the leadership could put simple elements in place to show support to ministries vital to the church culture. Is your leadership providing these ministry leaders the tools to reach their potential?

4. Is the idea of a "third place" something that could support the overall church vision? If so, what types of resources would be simple and efficient for your church to provide, in efforts toward creating a place where people frequent during the week?

    a. _____

    b. _____

    c. _____

    d. _____

5. During planning, there can be issues surrounding what ministries are allotted certain spaces. Asking this question can help resolve those situations: *"Does this [insert issue] speak the same language as the overall vision of the church?"*

   Here's an example: *"Does an investment in a commercial kitchen speak the same language as the overall vision of the church?"*

   Answer: *Do you have ministries actively working to feed large numbers of people on a regular basis? If not, you may be able to get by with a warming kitchen.*

6. What intrinsic qualities make up your church culture? How might these influence your needs for a space?

   _____

   _____

   _____

   _____

   _____

   _____

Recap: *Your vision needs to govern every decision you make. It will help you balance form and function. It will help you tackle the cumbersome yet rewarding job of creating a multipurpose space that will work for your church like your best soldier. It will help you draw people in, engage them, and then nurture them as you grow your church family.*

Chapter 2

PLANNING YOUR CHURCH'S FACILITIES

B y now, you have thought through the importance of your church vision and master planning, and you have a feel for the big picture of your goals for your future facilities. If you have put in the work to clarify your vision and think through how that vision will affect major areas of the church, you have a solid foundation to build on as you continue church planning. But what are your next steps, and what are the specific actions you need to take as you get started with turning your vision into a reality? This chapter will discuss the next stage of planning.

WHO WILL LEAD US?

Your single best chance at a successful project, no matter your financial situation or current attendance, is to appoint the strongest, most effective leadership team available. In small, elder-led churches or elder-led church plants, the elders and pastors commonly function as the building/facilities committee, appointing one person as the head (point of contact) for that group. Generally, however, once attendance reaches around 250 to 300 members, a separate group (building or facilities committee) becomes necessary since there is generally more pressure on the pastors' and elders' time.

Your single best chance at a successful project, no matter your financial situation or current attendance, is to appoint the strongest, most effective leadership team available.

Creating a building committee is not the same dynamic as acting as a committee-led church, although a committee-led church can certainly have a building committee (and they usually do). The building committee is a group who has been charged with managing church planning and making decisions within certain parameters set by the elders or pastors. The committee should consist of three to five people who are "in it for the long haul," as most building endeavors take an average of two to three years to design and build—and that's after the professionals join the party! In our experience, the ideal number of people is five because that number creates a diverse group of opinions which will initiate healthy conflict and strengthen your project over time. This number also allows the church to still be represented well even if all members cannot be present at every meeting. Within this group there should be a chairman who will act as the organizer for the group and will later serve as the first point of contact for hired professionals working on your project.

Note: *If your church does not currently charge one individual with long range planning for the church, you will want to consider this volunteer-based position. Good options for this position are elders, ministers, deacons, and/or members of the church with credible experience in the planning and/or construction industry. This person could be charged with monitoring the facility situation and approaching the leadership team when a matter needs to be discussed. You've probably heard the saying, "If everyone is accountable, then no one is accountable." It's a fact. This does not mean that the long-range planning head has authority over the future of the church's growth decisions; it means he is accountable for monitoring the matter and addressing it with the leadership. (As a side note, this is not the same person whom you'd charge with building maintenance or grounds upkeep—these are two very different positions.) This individual would also be an excellent candidate to serve as chairman of the building committee.*

Keep in mind that this committee is a group of people who will set the standard for the professionals later joining in with your project. These people will approve potentially very large sums of money being paid out to the people completing the work. They need to have their act together. This may sound harsh, but we are talking about best practices, efficiency, and avoiding confusion.

Many churches try to locate individuals with some background in construction or architecture to serve on a building committee. On the surface, it seems like a good idea. For example, the group below would be a stereotypical example of a building committee:

- Ron, retired mechanical contractor
- Linda, a stay-at-home mom with excellent taste in interior décor
- Joe, an accountant
- Veronica, who at one time was very active in the children's ministry
- Henry, a young man with some experience in landscaping

However, each of these people may or may not be an excellent member of this committee. Members who know something about wood framing, air conditioning, or colors actually have no advantage in this arena. Why? Because you can always call in a church member with experience in a certain area if you need them to consult on a challenging issue. In reality, the above group could be no more productive than this committee:

- Mike, an entrepreneur who travels frequently
- Brandon, a manager at a local grocery store
- Kristen, a physical therapist
- Clint, a banker
- Tara, a salesperson

The things that are important on a facilities committee are not always related to knowledge of construction or even good taste. For instance, the entrepreneur might actually be your best committee chair because he has experience in complicated, long-term projects and keeping a group on task. The woman in sales may also be excellent because her natural talent lies in uniting groups for a common cause. The retired man who was a mechanical contractor may be great because he's got some time and is respected as a quiet leader; or he might be a poor fit because he's known for spreading information prematurely. The stay-at-home-mom with great taste may be a poor fit because she may not be open to other member's preferences, or she might be great because in her past life she worked in finance and can help get your loan worked out!

Elders or pastors should each make a list of three to five prospective members who have suitable traits, and they should compare lists and select people mentioned more than once. Each committee member should add equal value to the group. Here's what to look for when making this list:

- Good business sense (Someone who has demonstrated success in strategy and execution of goals in general is a good choice.)
- Longevity with the church (A new member should not be a candidate for this position.)
- Strong relationships with multiple groups within the church body (Translation: Avoid asking people who specifically run in a "clique.")
- Tact when addressing others in the church and in the community (For example: A person known for frustrating or embarrassing people, even if unknowingly, is a poor choice for the building committee.)
- Respect for items that are sensitive or confidential (Translation: do not recruit a person known to be a gossip.)
- And finally, look for people with some snap—those who have a track record of thinking critically and making fruitful decisions in both their personal and/or professional lives and their ministry work.

Elders or pastors should each make a list of three to five prospective members who have suitable traits, and they should compare lists and select people mentioned more than once. Each committee member should add equal value to the group.

Aim for selecting critical thinkers who ask thoughtful questions and show good judgment, including the ability to know when to speak and when to listen. Their role is to ask questions until they understand situations, provide information, and make decisions. Choose the person, not the skillset. You will hire professionals to manage the work, but right now, you are looking for your board.

WHERE HAVE WE BEEN?

Before any specific actions take place, you need to have a straightforward conversation with your leadership team to define the story of your church. Surprisingly, knowing the story is not a given as much as some would assume. The older and more vibrant the history of a church becomes, the more that important details are likely to be lost. *Being able to tell this story factually and concisely, both verbally and graphically, will later give you the credibility to move your congregation to the next step.* This will help you in fundraising, in decision making, and in helping your church body feel ownership for your projects.

Your leadership team (and later your whole church) must know the whole story of your church and how that story relates to your facilities. Seeing the longevity of the church history and their future vision builds critical accountability and trust for the congregation. One can see this in the way that experienced pastors create capital campaign videos. Whereas a new church might ask the architect to create a simple video of the building model (which is always super exciting!), a more sophisticated approach is to integrate the building video as just a small part of a larger video that tells the following information:

- where the church has been (history of its beginning, its ministries, and its reach)
- where it is now (testimonials)
- where it's going (building model clip)

So instead of just being able to tell people what you are doing with the facilities, you will be able to clearly articulate the whole story of *why* and *how* you are doing it.

Before any specific actions take place, you need to have a straightforward conversation with your leadership team to define the story of your church.

To nail down your story, meet with your new committee (or elder body if you are a smaller group!), and define the phases of your church. Every single church is in a "phase" of their growth with regard to facilities. To a new pastor, the situation could feel like phase one, when the church has actually been through four phases already. The living room you first met in may have been phase one for you, and it is important.

Note: If you are at the onset of a church plant, the tasks listed here could feel extremely overwhelming. If you have very few members and virtually no leadership team in the season you are in, you need to create an advisory board of trusted individuals who will agree to participate in discussions with you about your church planning. No one is meant to make all of these decisions alone, or with members who are not necessarily qualified to take on strategic planning.

As more people become involved in your ministry, it's vital that every member of your leadership know the story backwards and forwards.

An open discussion about the major milestones of facilities you've been in is the first step. Maybe you, as a leader, already know this entire story, or you are a new church plant meeting in a living room with twelve people. As more people become involved in your ministry, it's vital that every member of your leadership know the story backwards and forwards. Discuss your story until you can be sure of two things:

1. Everyone knows and agrees on the same facts.
2. Everyone on your leadership team can easily tell this story to anyone who asks.

Check out an example of chronicling the history of your church's facilities in the tools at www.churchbuildingguide.com!

* * *

The church I grew up in is a good example of very successful long range facility planning. When I was 13, the church moved from a small neighborhood church that had held about 120 people to a new location that had formerly been a car dealership, just off a major highway. (This is one of four churches I've known to purchase car dealerships, and it works well.) So, here's how the chronology of this church's facilities evolved:

- *The neighborhood building was Phase I.*
- *Phase II was meeting in the showroom of the car dealership while using the adjacent car dealership offices for kids' classes, the service area offices for administrative offices, the break room for a kitchen, and the car make-ready shop as an unconditioned storage/ benevolence area.*
- *Phase III turned the car showroom into larger kids' classrooms, while adding on a new 300-seat auditorium (and leaving a large, open area available for a future auditorium expansion).*
- *Phase IV turned the make-ready shop into a big family life center with a kitchen, new restrooms, and youth gym. During the same project, a nearby metal building on site was converted into a great space for the clothing and food distribution ministry.*
- *Phase V was the renovation of the Phase III children's spaces, as the needs and numbers had changed over the past 15 years. At the same time, the original restrooms were renovated and expanded to provide additional stalls.*
- *Provided that growth continues, Phase VI for this church will one day be an extension of the auditorium to seat 350–500.*

The irony of this story, when I hear it from older members who remember every phase, is how "crazy" everyone said that the church leadership was for moving from the neighborhood church to the car dealership. However, the elders at the time had a long-range plan, and they worked hard to preserve the future possibilities during every phase.

WHERE ARE WE GOING?

So now you know, on paper, where you've been and where you stand. The next step is to define your current church needs. At any given time, a church has facility needs. Maybe you need an extra classroom or a playground. It could be that the foyer is less than welcoming. Or, maybe you're meeting in a living room, and at some point you will have to move out for lack of space. What are the spaces that need your attention now? Which needs should be put on a running list for future discussion?

Begin the habit of making a list of needs—both pressing and future. This is not to say you are discontent with your current situation, but you have made the decision to look ahead because a group of people have entrusted you with leadership. In addition to knowing your needs, you need to have a firm grasp of where you stand. Much in the same way that you need to know your monthly and yearly budgets, you need to know where you are in terms of how the number of people in your congregation relate to how much space you have access to.

> **What are the spaces that need your attention now? Which needs should be put on a running list for future discussion?**

Next, determine how much land you would potentially need as your church grows.

A good rule of thumb is that you'll need an acre for every 100–125 people (This rule of thumb does not work well when dealing with inner-city type groups operating in multi-story facilities, lease spaces where the church leases only a portion of the space, or churches meeting in homes).

Any extra land you acquire is positive as it can contribute to the church's assets as well as provide room for expansion. If your church does *not* own land, this rule of thumb can help you decide a range of land sizes to look for in your search.

Now, how much building do you need? This is not a cut-and-dried formula because churches need different things. However, go ahead and run the calculations through, and put an asterisk (*) beside your notes to remind you of the reasons why your situation may be unique; that information will be helpful down the road.

When determining the size of your worship space, allow about 25 sq. ft./person. "Worship space" is defined here as the main area of worship (the sanctuary), the baptistery, dressing areas, a foyer, and adequate restrooms.

To figure the size of a potential educational space, use 50 sq. ft./ person for small churches and 55 sq. ft./person for larger churches. Again—know who you are. If your church is heavily ministry based, and folks are working around the clock in all areas of the building, your situation is noticeably different from a church building typically used on Sundays until noon and on Wednesdays from 5:00–7:00 p.m.

To figure the size of a fellowship space, allow about 18–20 sq. ft./person, including the dining area, kitchen, storage, and some restrooms.

Go to www.churchbuildingguide.com to download a worksheet to help you with this step.

Knowing at any given time "where you stand" is power because you know the *specifics* of what you need. If I know I am looking for between two and three acres, I'm able to narrow down my choices and avoid wasting time. I can sort through the options critically and bring only truly viable options to the table for discussion.

I will always stand by this mantra in business, in parenting, and certainly in planning for churches: *The leader has to know the rules inside and out so that he or she feels confident knowing when to break them.* Maybe your church is located in the outer ring of a major downtown area and you are looking for three and a half acres to build a new building (or renovate an old one) and house major ministry operations. Clearly, land is pricey downtown, but one day you see two acres for sale at a price that catches your eye. If you know how much building square footage you need, you can probably work the numbers in the next 24 hours to consider a 2-story building on the property, or even an elevated building with parking below. At all times, the person or people in charge of the vision have to know where they stand and what their basic needs are for the future. If chasing down this info is in reaction to a potential opportunity, it's often too late. You're in charge of the vision, and you need to know where you stand. This puts you in a position to exhibit the very best stewardship in your decisions and react quickly to opportunities that would be in the church's favor.

> **The leader has to know the rules inside and out so that he or she feels confident knowing when to break them.**

Note: If you are in the phase where you are already vetting properties, it is time to enlist a professional for focused, simple services at an hourly rate to provide the information you need. Having an architect's team with all of your data on file that can quickly work through properties for you, using general assumptions and simple layouts, will save time and prevent costly mistakes. You, and certainly your leadership team, should never be charged with googling solutions or researching building codes. There is no reason to reinvent the wheel. Just ask for simple, reasonably priced services from people who know what to look for.

HOW WILL WE GET THERE? A CONVERSATION ABOUT FUNDRAISING

This is the section where we tell you how to raise millions so that you can build the place of your dreams. Laughable, isn't it? Actually, it's really not that funny. The pressure pastors face (and many times, they face this part alone) is real. In the very best of scenarios when the eldership and committees fully support the mission and carry a big portion of the work load, there is usually one person who has to get on the platform and make the case for a great deal of money: the pastor. No one likes to ask their membership for money, but there are ways to ease the burden, to avoid major disappointments, and to increase giving strategically for capital campaigns. (Because of the complexity of budgeting, we will discuss how to participate in balancing a construction budget in a separate chapter. This section is about the pastor and eldership's ability to fundraise.) In my experience, the churches that have had the best luck with fundraising are not necessarily the wealthiest congregations, but those with the best long-term plans.

Rule Number One of Fundraising: Keep the congregation updated with information you are sure of. It's tempting to tell the congregation every exciting detail of the work you are accomplishing in the planning process. However, the better approach is to update them regularly, but only with information you know with a degree of certainty. Here's an example of a very common announcement when a church has just purchased property:

"We are absolutely thrilled to announce we are embarking on the construction of a new building for the congregation! We have purchased land we never thought we could afford—praise God—and are in the midst of hiring an architect and contractor. We are interviewing four firms, all of which we know one way or another. Brother Smith is related to one of them—good luck Brother Smith! We are planning to be objective, but of course, our hearts are with your cousin's firm as he makes his presentation. Thanks be to God that a nephew of a member here in our congregation has volunteered his tireless services in designing the front of the building. You can see the rendering up on the screen. Wow, right? Unbelievable! And this fellow's only one year out of college; we couldn't believe it either. We have already approached the city with this picture, they luckily were okay with the rendering, and here's the floor plan we've agreed upon! As you know, these things aren't free [laughter from the audience], so we are beginning our campaign today in hopes of raising $1,000,000 within the next twelve months, this way we can move into the building right in time for Easter!"

I could pull many illustrations from the above paragraph. I could strike through every sentence that the pastor didn't actually know to be true. I could circle the information that should have been confidential. I could highlight items I knew would later spell disaster. But here's the point: in his own excitement, the pastor was misleading the congregation and setting himself up for several years of miserable announcements retracting statements he had no idea were not factual. Was it intentional? Absolutely not. Was it avoidable? 100%. In one five-minute announcement, the pastor said everything he could ever say to help fundraise for the next two years, and 90% of it was false. Here's what he could have said that day while still ensuring equal excitement:

"We are absolutely thrilled to announce we have reached a major milestone in planning for the future home of our church. We have purchased land we never thought we could afford—Praise God!" [Stop. This is a major milestone and the point of the announcement. This information is powerful.]

"Please begin to pray for our leadership as they enter the next phase of this project, which includes visiting with professionals who will help us reach our next set of goals. Also, begin praying about what your role will be in this project, whether that's to continue growing your ministries, contributing financially, or serving in another way. We will keep you posted!"

In the beginning, you are simply building excitement and letting your people know what's ahead! Think carefully and speak only what you know to be true based on solid advice, and not advice you've arrived at by means of hastily asked questions and badgering of people in the industry. The reputation of the project within the church needs to be above par at all times. There will be places in every journey where expectations are not exceeded, or timing is delayed. Construction happens outside the church body in a market that fluctuates like the wind, and there is no way to control every change. When things happen, you have to be able to get the congregational momentum to bounce back. Do not exhaust the congregation; simply keep them in the loop about milestones (positive or not so positive). It's all about sharing the proper perspective.

As a general rule, you want to update your congregation as much as possible about *why* you are pursuing a building project (e.g., growing ministries, growing needs, and growing kids). Then, of course show them *how* you are going to do it (communicating capital campaign goals and a running total of where you're at on the fundraising scale). And yes, as much as you can along the way, show them *what* you are going to do (using site plans, building renderings, etc.). So first deal with the *why*, then deal with the *how*, and then follow up with the *what*. This reinforces the role of the building and facilities as a *tool for your ministry*, not the other way around. In this manner, you are coaching the church into an intentional mindset about the project, where the building is clearly seen as a tool to support the work of the church. A church with such a mindset is much less likely to incur major disagreements over trivial parts of the project, because the focus is on the building as a tool, and the excitement lies there (as opposed to the color of a countertop, etc.).

As you begin work with an architect, ask them monthly if there is anything new you could show the congregation. The best practice is to wait until you have valid cost estimations before you present visuals of any kind, other than a very basic feasibility study (with which you would not mention a number that you need until you know that for sure). Keep the lines of communication open for questions, possibly through a comment box, which would be checked by the building committee chairman. Congregational questions should be discussed by the committee before answers are given, and the rule of thumb about sharing only the facts should be the general rule.

Many churches are hiring fundraising experts these days. These professionals can be an important asset, especially in very large congregations. The principles, however, are about the same:

- Keep the congregation updated on a very regular basis with facts about the project.
- Consider your position on whether you will accept pledges as part of your fundraising strategy, and if so, how you will redeem the pledges.
- Take time to explain to the congregation (usually the finance committee will assist with this) exactly how you are funding the project. If you have made the decision to borrow conservatively,

let the congregation know how and why you arrived at that decision. If you have decided not to borrow, you'll need to lay out those plans as well.

- Once design decisions have been made and prices negotiated/communicated, give the congregation access to flyers and booklets telling the wonderful news of what is to come!
- Strategize the best times to ask the congregation to consider major financial support. In the project schedule, there are some events proven to help fundraising: when people see the first drawing, and when the first backhoe shows up. Other great times are when the structure becomes visible and when you can take your congregation through their first building tour.
- Do not ask the congregation to support two ministries or efforts on the same Sunday, or even back-to-back Sundays. This does not benefit either cause. People who would have prayed and given to both causes will likely back off from one.
- We will discuss this in detail later, but there is a major difference between project cost and building cost. You need to tell the congregation how much the *whole project* is going to cost.
- Remember that people give to the church in two ways: time, and money. Chew on this: if someone is a major financial contributor, it is very likely that they are giving both time and money. If you don't actually see them at the church volunteering, they are still giving of their time in that it most likely takes them quite a bit of time to earn the money they are giving to you. Treat your ministry leaders and your major financial contributors similarly as it pertains to fundraising and you'll avoid a world of hurt feelings.
- On that note, consider how much "pull" you'll allow your ministry leaders and contributors to have about the details of the project. We recommend that all suggestions, regardless of whom they are from, run through the same channels. The building committee chair and the committee should discuss the suggestion and make a decision. If dispute arises about the decision, the elders should step in to resolve the issue.

> **Treat your ministry leaders and your major financial contributors similarly as it pertains to fundraising, and you'll avoid a world of hurt feelings.**

WHO TO ASK AND HOW

I want to step out of the role as architect for just a moment and into the role as a congregation member. Let's say my husband and I are sitting in church on Sunday, and they take collections for a new building. Our pastor tells us the church is working on a new building that will generate great improvements for church ministries and asks church members to please consider a donation if possible. Not a problem. My husband and I put $100 in the offering plate without needing to hear more detailed information.

In the grand scheme of a construction project, $100 is not a lot of money. If your church is going to be able to raise enough money for a building, people will need to donate in a major way, and you will need members to donate more substantial amounts. However, people who make larger donations have to be educated in a different way. Many people can place a $20 or a $100 bill in the offering plate based on one church announcement. If they're going to consider a larger donation, they need more information about what's going on. Where's the money going? Is this building going to be solid marble, and who is in charge of deciding what the needs are? People need to know what's going on before they will invest larger sums of money.

Here are some great ideas for communicating details of the project:

- Host a dinner or church-wide meeting to discuss what the project includes, how much it's going to cost, and how you are going to fund the project. (This event could be church-wide, or it could be reserved for ministry leaders and strong financial contributors.)
- If you are meeting monthly, ask your architect to bring a drawing item to show progress each month that you could show the congregation (requesting digital files is best, and you can print

what you need). The construction period is a little clearer as to the progress being made, but posting pictures and videos on social media, and using a hashtag for the project, is always helpful.

- Display large, high-quality image boards showing the project information in your current foyer or meeting space. (Ask the printer to dry mount the boards on half-inch foam core so they don't warp. It'll set you back about $200, but those bad boys will be sitting out there for a long while as you patiently await moving day!)

- Ask your architect's team to create a "Design Development book" for your presentation to key donors, financial contributors, or ministry leaders. Such a book might be spiral bound with a laminated cover and include information about spaces planned for certain ministries, what materials are planned for the building, a simple cost breakdown, and so on. This tool can be very special and useful as it might spark interest for individuals wondering where to donate their funds. (The pages of this book can also make a very effective slide presentation for a dinner or meeting event). *This item is a standard PlanNorth church project deliverable, and we love to create a digital copy for the church so that dozens of copies can be made as needed, or easily popped onscreen for a Sunday presentation. You can always request the same from your team.*

- Meet individually with specific financial contributors to present them with a copy of the book and thank them for their support of the church. Point out specific parts of the design where you think they may be interested in helping.

- Have your architect design a way to recognize people formally who have donated, large and small, in time or money. Dedication boards can be special pieces of the design, or a simple plaque with members' names written on small plates accomplishes the same goal. The thought is what counts here. Give people the opportunity to make even small donations in honor or memory of friends and family. Pass out forms with blanks stating "in memory of" or "in honor of" to help people consider how to honor loved ones.

- With today's technology, architects usually design in 3D. By the time you see what the building may look like, the building is usually modeled in 3D on computers. Consider having the architect make a quick animation of that model for you to set to music or merge with the rest of your campaign video. This is a typical service included in the cost of design at PlanNorth, and certainly at many other architectural firms as well. To take it a step further, you can even have the 3D model professionally rendered into a quality photo-realistic animation. A professionally rendered model typically looks absolutely real. These do come at some additional cost, so depending on your overall strategy you'll need to weigh the value.

- Consider large pieces of the project where you could offer naming opportunities for significant donations. For example, good options might be the children's wing, the kitchen, a distribution center, a youth gym, or meeting/adult classrooms.

- A word to the wise: have your architect (or a church member with some design skills) come up with a strategy for what the items related to the project are going to look like. In other words, *brand your efforts*. Branding helps people subconsciously understand that they are receiving the same message about the project. Every pamphlet, board, and digital presentation should look like it came from the same place because it bears the same message and the same graphics.

- Create nice "thank you" cards with that branding and put one leader (pastor or building committee member) in charge of sending handwritten, sincere thanks to every person who donates financially to the project.

- Let your community know what is going on! Get on social media and talk about your missions, your ministries, and what's to come. Tell the community what ministries you are serving by building/ renovating this new space. Tell them what's in it for them! I once heard a pastor say that they didn't like to be boastful about what they were doing, but sharing information is not being boastful. How can people help if they don't know what's going on? For example, if there's a new food pantry coming that's part of your new building, there could be someone who has been wanting to get involved in that type of ministry. They could be a potential donor or, even better, a new member! Tell the community what you have going on. Oversharing here is beneficial.

Action Items:

1. *Meet as an elder/pastor group to discuss potential facility team leaders. Each person should bring 3-5 names to the table for discussion. Compare lists and select the names of people that surface more than once. Approach the individuals, and explain to them the value that they bring to the table as well as the importance of their understanding of the church vision and culture. Ask them to consider the responsibility seriously before agreeing to serve.*

2. *Jot down a couple of general goals/concerns that you have currently with regard to your facilities:*

    a. _____

    _____

    _____

    b. _____

    _____

    _____

    c. _____

    _____

    _____

3. *Download and start to think about the "Church Needs and Usage List" at www.churchbuildingguide.com.*

    Are the greatest needs on your list in alignment with your vision for the church body? For instance, are the most important ministries with respect to your church receiving the greatest percentage of energy and potential funds toward resources, or is something out of whack?

4. *Download and work to complete the "Church Building Chronicle" at www.churchbuildingguide.com.*

    You will need to research and record basic information about the phases of the church growth, such as the place the church was meeting, how many people the establishment could reasonably accommodate, and your max attendance in that space. If you are a new church plant, this may be very easy. If you are a new pastor or elder at an established church, creating this document will help you begin to think strategically about the growth of the church.

Note: *Understand that the goals of this exercise are to (1) help everyone to know the story backwards and forwards as it relates to the overall vision of the church, and (2) see tangibly how the past trends of the church can inform future decisions. This is also an excellent resource to provide to your architect.*

Discussion Topics:

1. What individual value could each potential member of the leadership team bring to the cause of creating a built environment for the church to live? Jot down some thoughts:

    a. Name: _____

    Value to the Cause: _____

    b. Name: _____

    Value to the Cause: _____

    c. Name: _____

    Value to the Cause: _____

    d. Name: _____

    Value to the Cause: _____

    e. Name: _____

    Value to the Cause: _____

2. In what ways have these individuals demonstrated knowledge, understanding, and support of the church's culture and mission? Have there been specific instances where you feel these individuals do *not* totally understand the culture of the church?

3. What possible meeting schedule best fits the vision of the church with regard to planning? *Note: For churches in early strategic planning, consider meeting weekly for one month to organize all data and complete the Action Items, and then meeting quarterly or as requested by the chair. When a project is in design or construction, a monthly meeting is most typical.*

4. What are some of the fundraising strategies that you felt like might work for your church? What are some that you are sure would not be a good fit, based on the culture of your church?

5. In what ways can you show equal favor to your largest financial supporters and your most valuable ministry leaders? What does your culture say about how much input individual congregational members will have in the everyday decisions about the planning and design of your building? At some point, it will be the church leaders' responsibility to set these parameters.

Recap:

You are looking for the people in your flock who have the gift of leadership. Once you pinpoint who these people are and approach them with the task of serving in this way, it is vitally important that they understand the full church story, and that they are striving for the same vision as the eldership of the church. Once you have your team in place, you are ready to charge them with some work!

Chapter 3

SEARCHING FOR YOUR CHURCH PROPERTY

I f your church already owns property for expansion, this chapter will serve more as a checklist to highlight items that may need further research. If you are meeting in a space that needs revitalization, this chapter will help you develop a plan based on the facilities you already have. You may need to do some retroactive investigation to make sure you can confidently make decisions and prioritize your needs. If you are planning to one day purchase or lease property for your church, you will want to use this chapter as your go-to resource until you close a deal.

Typically, churches who need the most help, but who can afford it the least, are in the very beginning phases of seeking a permanent place to call home. You might be meeting in a member's home, or leasing something that for various reasons isn't meeting your church's needs. You know you need to be working toward change, but you aren't sure where to begin. All sensibilities aside, the possibilities of where churches could meet are essentially endless. The question becomes whether the decision is financially prudent, provides possibility for expansion (if not, can be quickly sold or benefit the church in another way), and, most importantly, sets the stage for your culture to thrive.

Thinking about the vision for where your church body might live can feel overwhelming and can provoke two opposite responses:

1. Paralysis by analysis
2. Hasty action based on little or no reliable advice

Both of these approaches have a tendency to exhaust the leadership and the congregation. Indecision will result in your church reaching the point of bursting at the seams, while hasty action (which is often based on an urgency to show the congregation their funds are being used correctly) usually results in poor decisions and disastrous consequences (typically financial in nature). A *conservatively proactive approach* is a much better strategy. Long before you are ready to hire any professionals or make a purchase, you have a lot of work to do to ensure that when the time comes, you can confidently strike while the iron is hot!

Have you ever thought, "Could someone just tell me if this property would work, how fast I could get it, and how much it would cost?" It's no secret that dealing with leasing and purchasing property is complicated and can move quickly! If you could quickly determine if a scenario is even feasible, you could save money and time. This is where feasibility studies come in. They are the fastest and most cost effective way to weigh a customer's options. For example, say we have a potential property we are considering, and we are wondering if it will work—can we get the parking spaces we need; can we seat all the people; can we have band practice; can we accommodate the food distribution ministry? And, importantly, does this property offer a reasonable price point, as compared to our other geographically acceptable options?

A **feasibility study*** can also figure out how your current facility could be expanded to meet your congregation's growing needs. Or, the study could compare your current location to a different one, with regard to space and price. A feasibility study could look at leasing versus buying.

---

* **Feasibility study**—a concentrated effort to determine whether an idea is financially, strategically, functionally, and aesthetically feasible. This study typically involves a design team working for a short time to address one or more possibilities (sometimes for land purchases and other opportunities).

Such a study is the quickest tool to help you make decisions about your next move. A feasibility study does not go into great detail, but rather investigates the major considerations of a location, leaving the smaller items to study later.

> A feasibility study can also figure out how your current facility could be expanded to meet your congregation's growing needs.

Feasibility studies are the single best value product offered at Plan-North because they offer the church a chance to compile all of the facts in a straightforward way, bringing clarity in preparation for good decision making. Knowing what to ask for will help you to get the correct information as well.

You are always in a place of advantage if you are armed with a detailed understanding of how your church needs stack up against a potential option for a facility (be that new construction or a renovation). Feasibility services are something my team routinely provides, and the time frame for small services such as this can be relatively quick. The prices for these types of services range from a couple of hundred dollars to a couple of thousand depending on the size of the property and the specific question. When contacting a professional for help on a feasibility study, be very clear with him or her about what your actual questions are. For instance, "Should we move here?" is a different question from, "We are moving here. What are the challenges we are going to face with this property?" Being crystal clear about your objectives will allow the team to spend their time intentionally (in other words, charge you only for things that matter to *you*!).

I'M LOOKING FOR LAND

First, simply put your nose to the ground. This is free and essentially common sense. Start getting a feel for the pulse of your target area as it pertains to commercial real estate. Subscribe to the local MLS listings (which will provide data about properties for sale) and follow all local realtor pages on social media (or just put them in your web surfing favorites if you are somewhat diligent about your online activity). If you have trusted realtors in your church, residential or otherwise, let them know what you are looking for so they can bring new listings to your attention quickly.

As you look through properties, you will begin to notice some patterns about your reactions to properties in relation to specific location. The goal should be to get to a point where you can draw a circle around a geographic area where you could "live." (Most of the time, this won't be an actual "circle.") While you are entering this phase, also begin to note property specifics that are essential to you. For example, in a downtown area, it may not be essential that you have your own building, or that you even own it! Long-term leases in heavily dense areas are very common and effective. A long-term lease in a rural community does not make as much sense (more on this dilemma later in this chapter). When you've got this pinned down, and it's time to get serious, hire the best commercial realtor around, not your friend or church member. Try to be objective— if you have a church member who's a great commercial realtor, go for it. But saving on fees is not worth losing the right piece of property.

The next step is to understand that your role is to evaluate the properties brought to you by your realtor. Of course, look at properties yourself, but if your realtor is good, they should see most new properties before you do. Give your realtor a checklist of information you need in order to evaluate properties (Go to www.churchbuildingguide.com to download a checklist for this step).

These properties are going to be harder to evaluate than, say, looking for a house. There are so many things to consider, and having the realtor complete the checklist beforehand lets you know at a glance how feasible the property is in very general terms. Otherwise, you will spend your time chasing down loose ends. Credible realtors have an excellent skillset for answering these questions. So, email this checklist to the realtor, and let them know that for each property you look at, you will need answers or direction before you will be able to pursue anything further.

Let's discuss some of the items on the checklist. Some may pose a challenge if you don't understand what they are and why you need them.

SURVEYS

Everyone knows you need a **survey*** in order to purchase property. What some do not understand is that there are many types of surveys. The most basic type is a **boundary survey**: this is a drawing showing the exact size of the property and the location of the pins already in the ground which indicate the boundaries. It shows who currently owns what, what the dimensions are, and sometimes states the **setback requirements** (the distance any structures on the property must be from adjacent roads). That's about it. If you're buying a house, boundary surveys are usually sufficient, but they are usually not adequate for a commercial property. An electrical, pipeline, or utility easement you did not know about can bring your plans to a screeching halt, even post-sale. Stating a rule of thumb for survey pricing without knowing the acreage or area is difficult. But without fail, the number will be in the thousands, not in the hundreds. Anything less than $1,000 indicates the information is not being researched or documented. Here are some things you need on your survey prior to purchasing the property:

1. Utility lines and easements
2. Electrical service location and type
3. Metes and bounds
4. Trees and topography (Note: This element of a survey can be put off until after the land purchase, but if you are sure you are buying the property, get it done. It will save you money to get it done upfront.)
5. Sewer/septic lines and easements
6. Grades (This aspect will look at the steepness of your site. This is important because you have to make sure patrons in a wheelchair can get up on the sidewalk and into the front door at a very low slope. Also, you want to avoid cars bottoming out and need gentle, reasonable slopes where water will drain practically and not cause flooding).

---

* survey—a general term to describe the documentation of a property's overall elements.

7. Water
8. Flood plain indications (100- and 500-year)
9. Highway right of ways
10. Pipeline or railway easements
11. Flood control easements due to existing elements adjacent to the site, such as bayous or other infrastructure

👍 A good rule of thumb is to get three quotes on survey services.

Ideally, if you know who your architect or civil engineer is going to be, ask them to secure the survey for you. They can get quotes for surveys and check over the work for you. Plus, if you need additional work later, the surveyor will know upfront that the architect or engineer will be contacting them and will be inclined to do a thorough job the first time.

If you are operating on your own at this stage, ask an architect, engineer, or contractor at your church what surveyors they know, and contact those surveyors. When you call, ask immediately if they typically provide surveys for residential or commercial. If they say both types, fine. But if they say residential, move on. The price for a residential-type survey will be deceivingly cheap, and you'll be sucked into purchasing info you can't count on later. Residential surveyors can be great at what they do, but you need a different type of information here than what they specialize in.

The survey team will need your (or the owner's) permission to enter the property. They will complete on-site work and let you know if they have any difficulties, such as the inability to locate pins. Surveyors will research easements and other information and will submit documents to you usually within a short time frame. If time is of the essence (for example, if you have a seven-day investigation period), make that clear when getting the quotes. Be sure to leave yourself some time to review the document carefully (with an architect or engineer), and request the file in two formats: a sealed PDF, and an editable AutoCAD or Revit file (these files are created on computer-aided drafting programs for building and site design).

Visit www.churchbuildingguide.com to borrow our form for this step.

THE GEOTECHNICAL REPORT OR "SOIL TEST"

Another item you will need is a soil test. This is the same item as the **geotechnical report*** or "geotech." People sometimes refer to this information as a "boring" or a "core boring." The purpose is to find out the bearing capacity the soil has—that is, how much the soil can hold up. Soils have different properties (some are sands, some are clays, etc.), so they possess different abilities to hold up structures like buildings. When you are adding any type of new construction, you will need a soil test. Also, if there is concrete being poured for anything other than a sidewalk (yes, this includes even the smallest of parking lots), you have to get this done.

To accomplish this, have a geotechnical testing company with a lab access your site with a drilling rig. If you aren't familiar with what this looks like, google "drilling rig." It is not a small piece of equipment. The company will bring their rig out to your site and will drill a shallow boring where you are likely to put pavement, like a sidewalk or driveway, and deeper borings (25 feet or so) where you are likely to place your building. They will then take these samples of dirt to their lab, and evaluate the properties of that soil.

Many people wait to conduct these tests until after the property has been purchased. You'll need to use good judgment here. Some of the cases where you need soil testing before purchase are:

- Pieces of property that are "unbelievably" cheap
- Areas where soil capacities vary greatly in a very small area (such as cities where some sites have sand and others have clay)
- "Tight" pieces of property where the development will have to be very dense to fit all the needs in.

Again, ask advice from your architect or civil engineer in this situation. If you have this person available, it's also wise to have them

---

* **geotechnical report** (or, soil test)—samples of dirt (also called "core samples") taken to determine the structural bearing capacity of the soil; that is, how much weight the dirt can sustain. The results of this test will tell you what type of foundation the building will need (slab on grade, piers, etc.).

handle soil testing so they can look for circumstances like the bulleted examples above. Ideally, the architect would send the geotech company a drawing of the site with the boring locations marked so that they can drill close to where you may build.

Depending on the drilling company's schedule (again, ask about this upfront!), you'll receive a report explaining the properties of the soil and the recommendations for the building foundation. They will recommend items such as "piers," "structural slabs," or certain types of beams and a slab on a grade. They will recommend the size of the rebar (a steel reinforcing rod which goes in the slab), and they'll tell you whether your dirt is sufficient to build a slab on or whether you'll need to bring in better dirt (select fill). If you do not yet have an architect or engineer on board who can translate the findings for you, sit down with the geotechnical company and ask them to explain in laymen's terms what they are recommending. A recommendation of a structural slab, for instance, means the soil is in poor shape, and your foundation will be more costly than average. This information is relative to your setting: if you are in a dense city area, you have limited options, but if you're in the country, you have more options. Knowledge of the facts in all areas is key. If your foundation is going to be costly, it's not a deal breaker, but it is something you need to know upfront.

ENVIRONMENTAL TESTING

Speaking of knowing things upfront, many people have the same geotech company also test for contaminants (environmental testing). Environmental testing is not required in all jurisdictions, and *certainly not on all properties*. A city authority or your architect can tell you whether any environmental testing is required.

If environmental testing is required, it is prudent to do that prior to the land purchase. Brownfield sites, or sites with environmental issues requiring remediation, can be very expensive to handle. There are government incentives and grants in some cases, but these types of scenarios are very specific and have the potential to cost large sums of money. If the results indicate issues of any kind, you would be wise to make 100% sure you understand what the problem is and what it will cost to remedy. You can ask the testing agency for the names of several companies who can correct the problem, and then contact them directly for a quote. Some environmental issues are minor (someone dumped trash a year ago); others are totally prohibitive. Do not purchase property until you have a clear picture of what you are dealing with.

DETENTION

Will you need to reserve room on your site for detention? How much, and where on the site? Almost all city jurisdictions require detention, and very few churches accept this without argument. People usually have reservations because they do not want to turn a large part of their property into a space that cannot be used for facilities. It seems unfair to have to pay for the land and then not use it. But commercial property owners (like churches) are required to put in detention so that their development does not cause additional flooding to the overall infrastructure of the city.

Here's the logic on detention: when land is raw dirt, rainwater soaks back into the dirt pretty quickly. When that land becomes surfaces like roofs and concrete parking lots, the water doesn't soak in but runs out to the street and causes flooding. Detention ponds, as opposed to retention ponds, are not meant to hold water. A detention pond's function is to catch water temporarily and slow the runoff while releasing it slowly back into the watershed. The denser your city is, the more the city will be highly sensitive about detention requirements. To find out what your requirements are, ask your architect or civil engineer (preferably both) to have a conversation with the city engineer. Detention will be required unless you live in a very rural area or are purchasing a large piece of country property. In this case, you should still have a meeting with the local authority to ask. If you are in the city, the local authority is your city engineer. If you are not in the city limits, you need to contact the county.

We sometimes tell leaders to sketch out what they *think* is a reasonable amount of land to use for detention and then multiply that number by 3 ½. Just kidding—but the amount will be greater than you think. Some detention can go in lower parking areas and ditches. If you are in a seriously high-density area, you can even consider going underground with your detention. Underground detention strategies are very common in urban areas although they carry a significant cost increase.

At our company, we like to take a conservative approach to detention. Find out what the city requirement is and meet it—and that's all. If a city authority tells you or your team (I'm speaking from direct personal experience here) detention is not required, you need to get that conversation into a signed letter from that authority. When you request this paperwork, you may learn that the individual may not have that authority after all, at which point you'd need to find out who is in charge and converse with them directly, in writing. The best practice is to have your architect or civil engineer confirm these requirements.

Many churches approach detention with the feeling that the city will treat a church differently than another commercial establishment, but this is not so (more on this topic in a later chapter). In the eyes of a city official, a church is a large group of people meeting in a place, and they have the same needs as the next community member. Would it be fair for your neighbor, a small business owner, to have flooding on his property because of the amount of concrete you need on your site? No, and there are no churches I know who would willingly cause harm to their neighbor. Detention is a pain to some, but it's the right thing to do on all accounts.

👍 **Rule of Thumb:** *You must have detention for any new building or paving improvement, and your property will need more than you think.*

The final authority on this is the city engineer in your jurisdiction who is in charge of civil development, and the person on your team who will design and seal the drawings for your detention pond will be your civil engineer. Your civil engineer is a member of the architect's team, so if you can't understand the engineer's terminology, the architect can translate for you.

LOCAL AUTHORITIES

At some point, you will need to find out who is in charge of deciding what and how you can build. Architects and engineers are usually the best people to take charge here; finding out this information from city authorities is a daily task for them and typically much easier for them to accomplish. However, if you need to run with this yourself, go to your city's website and click on "building permits" or "planning and development." Find a phone number and call the department. Let the receptionist know you are looking at a particular piece of property on which to build a church and ask to speak to someone who can help you decide if the property is zoned for use by a church. Be very clear that this property is specifically for a church. A city official will examine your zoning and approve your plan for a church facility in that location. (For the sake of efficiency, you might consider adding this task of confirming certain items to your realtor's checklist). If the property is not zoned for church use, you will either need to pass on the property or consider the likelihood of obtaining a **variance*** which would allow your church to use the property. The larger and more sophisticated the city, the more you might consider enlisting professional help with these tasks. Early-phase city communication is a good example of a simple, professional service of great value to a church during planning.

If you are able to make a personal contact at the city, especially if you are in a small town, you might be at an advantage. They may help you later on when you are navigating the waters of city permitting. But do not put all of your eggs in that basket. City officials are regular people, who work in one of the most difficult arenas. They take new jobs (frequently), they move to positions where their authority changes, and they forget conversations from years past (because they have these types of conversations daily). You need to do your very best to keep a paper trail of conversations, so that you are organized and making decisions

---

* **variance**—a requested deviation from a city's typical code understanding/enforcement (Ex: "The movie theater requested a variance at the council hearing because they wanted to install a much larger than average pole sign.").

based on their input. An engineer's or architect's upfront input here will be very valuable to you.

At the end of the day, local authorities will do what they believe to be in the best interest of the city jurisdiction and their job. Period. The nature of their job is to review and enforce your project for compliance with government codes. Until that time when you receive a building permit, it's just talk. Getting conversations in writing when you are discussing requirements is mandatory, and those conversations should take place between the city and your Architect of Record, with you copied, so that the professionals are also involved and nothing is lost in translation. But even so, the idea is approved only once you have the building permit in your hand.

IN THE EYES OF YOUR LOCAL CODE ENFORCER

City officials look at buildings a little differently than the public, and even a little differently than architects and engineers. While architects and engineers will reference codes to complete our overall design goals, the entirety of a city building official's career is based on codes. Sometimes churches expect to be granted at least some degree of leniency on items such as parking, fire sprinkler system requirements, detention, and other code-mandated items. The truth is that the city officials do not see your church as a loving group of people serving and sharing. They see it as a type of building, and that's their job. While they may admire what you are doing personally, their professional responsibility is to zero in on what you are building and confirm that your design team has applied the correct codes.

What you are required to provide and do in a space is based on something called "Occupancy Type." Occupancy type is basically a description of what you are planning to do in the building and involves various categories. Some examples include Mercantile, Business, Industrial, and Assembly. Church worship spaces are designated as Assembly. In simple terms, Assembly spaces are places where people gather in groups.

So if you are moving into an old church and renovating, you are not changing the Occupancy Type of that building. If you are moving into an Office Building and turning it into a Church, you are *changing the occupancy type* from Business to Assembly. If you are moving into another type of Assembly space such as an Event Center, you will be closer in requirements, but there are several types of Assembly Spaces. Even though it's the exact same actual building, the *purpose* of the building is what determines what the codes are going to require. Do not assume you can move in without building more parking, more restrooms, putting in detention, etc. This is something that the architect will check during their code search, or you can bring those questions up to the city prior to the land purchase, if you do not have an architect helping you at that time.

Let's think like a person who is charged with making sure the building is safe (a city official, for example). Say I am in charge of multiple projects, and I am actually inclined to bend the rules a bit. Which project would I bend the rules for: the office building with four employees, or a church building with 300 occupants? If I were inclined to bend the rules, it would be for the small project. While you might think, "They should know we have no money! We are a church doing the Lord's work!" they are only seeing the number of people involved. An Assembly space has higher code requirements because the health, safety, and welfare of many people is at stake. And frankly, that's for the best. As a leader in your congregation, it is strongly in your best interest to adopt the same philosophy. You must have an architect who understands the intent of the codes so that you can meet the codes and then move on. *You do not need someone looking to be the teacher's pet of the city permit office.* City officials respect professionals who do their own code research and can explain their reasoning. Every once in a while you run into a problem and you have to pick your battles. Respect and professionalism, as well as compromise, are key on all sides.

PARKING

Many times, the amount of parking a church needs (either to meet code or for their own use) is actually the biggest driver in determining how much land is needed. Most often, regulations require church facilities to provide one parking space for every "x" number of seats. One parking space for every 3 to 4 seats is a common ratio. Whether or not you are using fixed or moveable chairs is a factor which will come into play here. If you don't yet know what your plans are for the seating, your architect should figure it both ways and plan for the greater of the two (at least in the early planning stages).

For moveable chairs, the square footage of the sanctuary usually determines the parking requirement, instead of the seat count. While it's not really reasonable to figure the exact number of chairs that will fit in a sanctuary you haven't designed, you can certainly estimate the number. When you know those two items (the square footage of your sanctuary and the number of people you plan to seat), you can ask your architect and/or your city official what the general requirements will be.

If you are concerned that room for parking may be an issue, investigate whether the city allows shared parking agreements between neighbors. Some cities even make it a part of their own codes, which is usually greatly in a church's favor (The Woodlands, Texas, is one example). Churches are prime candidates for these agreements because the typical hours of a church are different from the typical hours of most businesses. Don't be afraid to go to a potential neighbor and ask—most people are receptive to the idea and appreciate the idea of keeping their lots in use during off-hours for safety reasons. So then you can partner up with your neighbors and say, "Okay, you're not open on Sundays. We are open on Sundays. Can we agree on paper that your customers and employees can park in our lot during the week, and we can park in your lot on Sunday morning?" Occasionally people are a little antsy about the liability, but usually they favor the arrangement.

> **If you are concerned that room for parking may be an issue, investigate whether the city allows shared parking agreements between neighbors.**

EXISTING BUILDINGS

If you are looking at sites with buildings on them, you will need to vet these sites in a completely different manner. (Note: if you are working on a church revitalization, this is also a useful section for you!)

While existing buildings may save you some time, you will have quite a bit more investigation on the front end. To recap a bit from previous sections, you'll need to confirm that the city will let you use these buildings for a church. If they are already functioning as a church—great, you should be in good shape. Renovations are often exciting because it's so much easier to visualize options, as opposed to starting from scratch, but you need to keep a clear head and limit your excitement until you've checked off some key boxes. Ideally, you need to walk through potential buildings with your design and construction team and confirm the degree of complexity of the situation you are walking into. Doing this prior to making an offer is smart.

THE EXISTING BUILDING'S STRUCTURE: METAL

The next thing to do is to make note of the building's structure. Metal buildings with large, open spans make good worship spaces. What's nice about buildings with a metal structure, pre-engineered or not, is that they usually have large spans. What can be a challenge is working around the large metal columns in some of the areas like classrooms, offices, and foyers. Columns in the middle of the potential sanctuary area create a significant challenge, but occasionally this problem can be remedied with creative seating layouts or by installing strategic beams to lengthen the distance between columns.

Warehouses and barns with open areas that can be "closed in" are not necessarily a good option because warehouses are not usually structurally designed for church use. Those structures typically cannot handle the weight of ceilings, lights, stage lights, and so on. If you plan to add ceilings in any areas, technology such as projectors, sound equipment, or lights, the building needs to be evaluated by a structural engineer. Because a structural engineer's investigation fee might cost about $1,500 to $5,000, this cost will be a good investment only if the building seems like a good fit in all other ways. Most of the time, what you would spend retrofitting these structures could have purchased the foundation and structure of a new building. What's the point here? Do not assume that a warehouse or a barn was designed to support anything other than a tin roof. There's a 95% chance it was designed to do exactly what it did in the first place.

THE EXISTING BUILDING'S STRUCTURE: WOOD

Wood framed buildings can also be a good fit, but they come with challenges: finding a large enough space to hold services, and then making sure the ceiling in that area is high enough for an acceptable worship experience. Wood-framed buildings are structural in nature: that is, the wood itself is bearing the load of the roof. Do not walk through a wood-frame building saying, "We'll blow out this wall and that wall, and we'll take out the ceiling and just spray paint the area black." This type of project will be a puzzle even to your design team because of the type of support the walls and ceiling must have. A good team will dig in and offer you a feasibility study of your options, but it'll involve some real investigation by various trades (structural and mechanical engineers, to name a few). If you've got your eye on a deal, and the deal is a wood-framed building, walk through the building with your architect and, ideally, your construction manager.

ASBESTOS*

Most likely, as you walk through your potential new space, your team will mention that you need an asbestos inspection. An asbestos inspection is required for all buildings unless an Asbestos Free Certificate can be produced. When you are negotiating the property, you will want to request that the seller produce this document. Some can and some cannot. If the building is less than 20 years old, the seller may have it on file or could call the general contractor who built the building. If the building is much older than that, you'll likely have to have an inspection done.

The law states that in order to begin any type of demo or construction on an existing building, you must produce one of two things: (1) an Asbestos Free Certificate stating that at time of construction there were no asbestos-containing materials in the building, or (2) proof that a current asbestos inspection was completed (i.e., a report).

---

* **Asbestos**—a mineral-type material composed of thin fibers and used widely during the 20th century for construction and buildings. It is now commonly known to cause illness and fatality through exposure, and has been banned for construction purposes.

Asbestos inspections run in the $2,000 to $8,000 range for most buildings, funds that can be saved if you have the certificate that says the building is Asbestos Free. If the current owner does not have this document, you are required by law to test the building prior to beginning any construction. Once you receive the results, hopefully you are in the clear. If not, it's important to understand the difference between harmful asbestos and asbestos that is unlikely to be harmful.

There are two types of asbestos: friable and non-friable. Friable asbestos is harmful because it can be airborne and enter your body.

An example would be sheet rock or ceiling texture which contains asbestos—if you have asbestos in sheet rock or ceiling texture, it's most likely friable asbestos. (Again, this is not a test you would do yourself; this would be part of the testing agency's scope of work). At the end of their testing, the agency will give you a formal report which you in turn will turn over to the city prior to obtaining your building permit. If the asbestos is non-friable, such as a glue in a floor tile, then by law it can be covered. It cannot be left open. My recommendation, however, is that you have all asbestos cleaned out of buildings no matter what the cost, or go to another building. Future generations should not suffer in the event that there is information about asbestos, even non-friable, that we do not yet know. People used to think cigarettes were safe. We still have much to learn about materials and chemicals.

OLD BUILDINGS

In a very old building, you have to approach the situation with a different mindset than with newer structures. In a 20-year-old building, for example, you can walk in wondering if there's asbestos. In a 50-year-old building, however, you are *expecting* asbestos, foundation issues, roof replacement, HVAC replacement, electrical reworking, and possibly mold and plumbing problems. Buildings were once typically thought to have a "50-year lifespan." In most cases, that's accurate. Do not let this deter you from renovations, but do enter the arena with the knowledge that there is a major difference between renovating a 10- or 15-year-old building and a 40-year-old building. In many cases, renovating can be every bit as expensive as new construction, and sometimes even more costly. If you go to a contractor and ask them for a ballpark price to renovate an older building, you will most likely experience some sticker shock. Working in "reverse"—that is, going back and remediating layers of code issues, structural concerns, environmental problems, and the like—is costly.

So why on earth would anyone do this? Actually, there are many reasons. Maybe geographic location is critical, and your options are very limited. Or, perhaps you own a very old building and need to create a phasing plan to revitalize the property over the course of several years. If you own an old building or church campus, you will need to assess the property as a whole (considering all factors mentioned), and work with your architect to develop a phasing plan to get the campus into shape without overwhelming the membership financially and emotionally.

> In many cases, renovating can be every bit as expensive as new construction, and sometimes even more costly.

When surveying old buildings, have the basic expectation that things will need to be repaired on all accounts. In addition, you probably need to be prepared that the situation is likely to become very stressful. There is a difference between knocking out some walls in a 10 or even a 20-year-old building, even if there are structural considerations, and dealing with a building much older than that.

REPURPOSING BUILDINGS

What if you find a building that's currently used for a purpose other than the one you need? For example, perhaps you want to take an old car dealership and turn it into a church. Great idea. This is known as repurposing, and it's actually pretty noble to consider this approach, along with sometimes being a good deal financially.

First, realize this is not the same task as renovating a big, open area, and it's not the same as moving into an existing church. Repurposing is admired because it's a challenge, but be aware that it can be more difficult and more expensive than renovating an already existing church building. Before you start thinking about knocking out walls, remember to consider city regulations. You will need an architect to run the codes and, in a set of drawings, explain to the city that the structure would be changing occupancy type. Armed with the understanding that the building may need additional restroom fixtures, more parking, and possibly even a fire sprinkler system, you can then determine whether it's still a good option.

If you have even a couple of weeks to consider such a scenario, you should then request a set of as-built drawings from the current owner, if they have them. Most of the time, they have something, even if it's not totally accurate. If not, you might seriously consider having an architect's team do some quick measurements and get it into AutoCAD (a drafting program that will generate two- and three-dimensional drawings). Architects can usually complete these tasks fairly quickly as a simple, hourly service.

> **Would the culture and vision of your church be best served by renovating a structure, constructing a new building, or by repurposing a space?**

Once you have drawings in hand (or sometimes even as you walk through), you can start to determine if the building would work for you. All requirements and regulations aside, you have to give serious thought as to whether this building would work for your unique needs and culture. Can you get some reasonable ceiling height for worship? Are the materials going to be an acoustical challenge, and would there be solutions? A feasibility study in this case would work to answer all of those questions so that you can make an educated decision. Should you decide that it would work out, this drawing from the study might be the first thing you present to the congregation to cast your vision for this new step.

Would the culture and vision of your church be best served by renovating a structure, constructing a new building, or by repurposing a space? Would a very specific location serve your church vision most effectively?

ACCOMMODATING THE DISABLED

Another aspect to consider is whether the previous owner met the state-required accessibility laws for disabled people (commonly referred to as "**ADA**"* regulations). Architects can tell you generally where you stand on this as they walk through a building, or you can hire a RAS (registered accessibility consultant) to tell you exactly how "far off" the building might be. Because this particular code is updated very frequently, almost all buildings being sold would need at least minimal upgrades. Very old buildings would likely need a total overhaul, considering items like ramps, clear space, grab bars, reaching ranges, and others. Major accessibility upgrades can be very expensive, but accessibility in new construction is at almost zero additional cost (this is one more reason renovations tend to be costly). Today, commercial construction managers try very hard to have these costs built into the cost of the project from day one.

One additional note—the actual worship spaces (sanctuaries only) are exempt from the ADA. However, there is not a church out there who shouldn't consider the needs of the disabled. Providing spaces for wheelchairs in the sanctuary (in several different locations) is not only thoughtful, but it's the right thing to do, and other disabilities should be considered as well.

LEASING VERSUS BUYING

Let's think about what types of people lease a house. The first type of person who leases a house is a person who cannot afford to buy a house. The second type of person who leases a house is someone who needs flexibility to change locations. They may be able to buy a million-dollar home, but they're going to lease an apartment because next month they may want to live somewhere else. Additionally, someone might lease because of the lack of availability of properties for purchase in their desired area (for instance, high density city areas). Related to this

---

* **ADA (American Disability Act)**—the law which requires all new construction and renovation projects to make provisions for handicapped persons to use a building in a reasonably equal way to a non-handicapped person.

scenario is a fourth type: someone who determines a long-term lease is financially and operationally superior to buying in their situation. So, do you fall into one of these categories?

Are you working toward financial stability and currently cannot afford to purchase property, but you long to own your own building one day? It might make sense for you to lease and work your way up. When you're negotiating the length of your lease, look back at your church growth. For instance, maybe you've grown *x* percent every year, and your giving has increased *y* percent for each of those years. If you can chart these numbers as they relate to each other, you could make a projection that will answer this question: If we're still leasing, because that's what we have to do, then at what point would we be ready to buy something? This situation is very similar to leasing in hopes of buying a home—you will need to pay rent and at the same time save for a down payment. If you are going to lease temporarily while you prepare to buy, you need to spend the minimal amount of money that you can get by with during this phase while still feasibly building your culture and vision. You need the location to be clean, inviting, comfortable, and acoustically pleasant. Past that, you don't need to invest in anything that cannot easily be moved to your permanent home one day—consider this when you purchase stage and light equipment, furniture, and other items. Have an objective couple of members tell you the truth: if the place looks disgusting, you'll need to do a fresh coat of paint. Weird smells must be addressed, or flagged as a deal breaker. Those types of items are not worth losing potential members, but fight the urge to get carried away on spending in this situation.

Rule of Thumb: One of the best strategies I've seen in budgeting is to save the "fifth Sunday" contributions for long-range planning purposes.

Some churches use this as a means to create a building fund, pay down a mortgage, save for a down payment on property, revitalize major portions of the existing facility, etc. Resist the urge to throw that money into maintenance, though. Maintenance should be a separately budgeted line item; this strategy is about future growth.

Are you looking at a lease because of reasons other than your inability to purchase—for instance, operational or geographical reasons? Sometimes this type of situation is the most difficult of all. You need to consider this lease space exactly as if it were something you own in terms of long-range planning, with one exception. You have to keep a tight hold on how much capital you invest in a property that does not belong to the church. Long-term leases ease this burden because you can certainly invest more if you are planning to stay for a long while. If leasing is really your long-term destination, you'll want to create the feeling of permanence for the congregation by laying out your vision for the spaces just as if they were your own. Permanence often involves investigating ministry needs, establishing budgets for major and minor improvements along the way, laying out plans for the time when membership grows (long-term leases *must* have capability for expansion), and growth milestones to celebrate along the way.

In this scenario, there may also be possibilities for subleasing certain spaces to organizations during the week to offset your costs.

FEASIBILITY STUDIES: HOW TO GET THIS DONE

Once you've found a piece of land or building you are vetting, you will need to complete a feasibility study.

I have yet to complete a feasibility study for a church who did only one study. This is the stage of the game where you are fleshing out ideas to see what sticks. Creating a feasibility study usually looks like this: an architect will take the prospective site image from Google Earth. Then, we will overlay all the survey info on the Google Earth image to scale. We will mark all the things we've been discussing: detention, easements, utilities, road access, etc. We will then draw a very simple indicator of the church's plan (example: a 20,000 square foot building and the associated parking lot). The layout would include appropriate turning radiuses, code requirements, etc.

We will draw in things we know will be factors later on, such as covered drop-offs, handicapped parking, and fire lanes around the building. We will leave as much room as possible for future expansion and mark it as such. In most cases, we will also start all over and come up with two to three other scenarios that might work on that site. Along with this image, there would need to be information about all the specific needs of your church that we have been discussing as well as how much the project might cost. You will not have a firm number at this stage, but you can establish the project budget *for that scenario*. A feasibility study is extremely useful because it can define how different scenarios would work and allow you to weigh your options in a whole new way.

Note: *You need to begin to think of these fixed variables mentioned here, such as easements and parking requirements, as facts. If a church purchases a piece of property without investigating if their facility will work long term, they may unfortunately be stuck making expensive concessions to work problems out. These types of situations can usually be worked out strategically after the fact for a price, but reinventing the wheel is rarely in a church's best interest financially. (Example: forgetting to consider detention when the city requires it, and having to put in an expensive underground detention system).*

If you are doing a feasibility study for an existing building, your study will look a little different (as we discussed earlier). It's more important in that case to show how the rooms will work in the building, for no other reason except to confirm that they do work out. This type of feasibility study would dig into whether you'd be required to build additional features to the building based on a change of occupancy or other factors, and generally how much that would cost. For new construction, those items aren't as important in a feasibility study because you have the freedom to define them during the design process.

> **A feasibility study is extremely useful because it can define how different scenarios would work and allow you to weigh your options in a whole new way.**

A feasibility study prior to land purchase is meant to accomplish one goal—to confirm or deny the viability of the property for your use (such that you can make a decision about whether to pursue the purchase). Once a property is purchased (building or land), you will continue planning and will enter the design phase.

Once your building committee has a reasonably good idea of how you will approach finding a space, be that land or an existing structure, you have reached a major milestone! Even if you have not made final decisions but you have ruled out many possibilities or reached consensus on the geographical search area, you have come far. Be sure to celebrate the little wins along the way, while staying mindful that there is still much work to be done.

Action Items:

1. *Confirm the specific geographical area in which your church could feasibly live. Mark this area on a map, and share with the team and your realtor.*

2. *Download the "Church Property Search Checklist" at www. churchbuildingguide.com, and edit the checklist to work for your needs. Make sure that your realtor has a copy if you have a property search or vetting effort ongoing.*

3. *Set up a facilities fund for the church. What strategies can you implement to build the funds in this account on a regular basis?*

Note: *Some of the uses for such a fund besides the costs associated with a building or renovation are preliminary planning needs, opportunities to vet potential properties, and feasibility studies which will all inform the leadership team so that good decisions can be made.*

Discussion Topics:

1. How could community-based partnerships, such as shared parking agreements and respect for local authorities, potentially work for or against your overall vision for the church?

_____

_____

_____

2. Is there anything specific about the culture or vision of your church which could be well-served by renovating a building

versus new construction, or by repurposing a space? (For instance, the desire to be in a very specific location or near a certain neighborhood).

_____

_____

_____

3. If you are considering leasing a space versus buying, what is your primary reason?

_____

_____

_____

What actions might be taken to work toward ownership, or, if that is not the goal, a permanent feeling in your leased space?

a. _____

_____

_____

b. _____

_____

_____

c. _____

_____

_____

4. What groups of people, specifically in your jurisdiction, are you trying most to serve? What fixed variables relating to those goals could serve as guides when deciding "where" you will live?

(Example: a church needing to be located within walking distance of a neighborhood, or near public transport with routes to and from the area they wish to serve)

Recap: *Where your church decides to live physically is a huge decision, and it should be based on the overall vision for the church. Educate yourself in a big-picture sense on the topics that will inform this decision, and know when to seek counsel on topics specific to the construction industry.*

Chapter 4

DESIGNING YOUR CHURCH'S HOME

Finally, you can figure out how this building will work! *Work* is the operative word here, because when it comes to churches, you need every space to function at full capacity for your ministries. In order to make this happen, you'll need to spend some time defining the problem before you jump into the possibilities. Again, remember to think about how the overall vision factors into these decisions.

PROGRAMMING

Would you like to be able to predict with some degree of certainty how large your building needs to be to accommodate your current membership and ministries and allow some room for growth? This information is critical to determining your budget, beginning fundraising, and getting into your new building. You don't want to overshoot the size of the building because your budget is likely a somewhat fixed product of what you can raise and what you can borrow. But what's the point of building something new if you are going to outgrow it before you move in?

Accurately predicting your church building's size is extremely important, because the single biggest driver of your cost is square footage.

We are always surprised at how quickly (and somewhat arbitrarily) many churches arrive at a square footage target for their building. Many times churches make this decision in reverse—for example, they strategize, "At x dollars a square foot, we can afford a 5,000 square foot building." But what if 5,000 square feet doesn't touch the needs of the church? A wise approach is to determine very early on if your needs are in the same range as your budget capabilities. If it turns out that the needs are *not* aligned with the budget in a realistic way, it is surely better to know upfront so that other strategies can come into play: phasing, leasing, temporarily locating certain ministries offsite, and so on.

> **Accurately predicting your church building's size is extremely important, because the single biggest driver of your cost is square footage.**

In a nutshell, **programming** is figuring out how many square feet you need to meet your needs. If money is no object, programming is a cinch. But if money is a concern—and it always is—programming is complicated because you will need to maximize use of every space. Even if you are not considering truly multipurpose spaces, your rooms will still be used for different uses when practical. Typically, when you first list out a church's needs and figure the square footage, the number is astronomical. But through careful analysis, we can determine a number that will truly work on all accounts.

In order to answer the question of how much square footage you need to build, an architect has to know the specifics of your church activities. What are your ministries? Do you focus heavily on world missions? How many children did you have over the course of the last couple of years, and how are you serving those children? Are you serving food to a thousand people every week? These things are second nature to you, but completely unknown to your architect, until you share your information.

Here is how programming works: first, we make an all-encompassing list of needs and uses. Then, your architect will assign square footages to those uses (a few rules of thumb are listed below). Once this list of basic square footages is created, we compare this list to the church's calendar to generally confirm which items should be tag-teaming and sharing spaces. The best practice for programming is to create the list of needs yourself, and then let the architect add his or her thoughts to the list in addition to assigning the square footage estimates. At that point, the team should meet together to brainstorm what ministries could and should easily share spaces. This is a meeting where the architect should mostly listen and take notes.

> **One of the best actions a church leadership team can take in this phase is to be crystal clear with the design team about what is really important, what it semi-important, and what is less important.**

One of the best actions a church leadership team can take in this phase is to be crystal clear with the design team about what is really important, what it semi-important, and what is less important. (In other words, identify items as a need versus a want.) That is extremely difficult, but that's one of the reasons why it is so important to have a strong, positive leadership team in place to help you. These people will need to keep the vision front and center as they decide where to invest the most square footage (read: money) in the design of the building. Armed with the knowledge of what the church needs and wants, and your wish list items, you can start to investigate each area individually. And that's very exciting! The remainder of this chapter will equip you with discussion points as you work on programming:

THE WELCOME SPACES

The notorious first impression! Your church parking lot, sidewalks, entry points, and lobby are your one and only chance to make that critical first impression. Fancy is usually of no use, but clean and welcoming are absolutely key. Also remember that people need to know where to go without much confusion. Here are some other considerations:

- Consider the lobby/foyer as a main hub. Once a person enters the building, there should be either obvious directional information or a nice signage plan to immediately let people know where to go. Remember to put yourself in the shoes of each type of person (for example, parents and children), and consider how they would experience the building (your architect should also do this).

- The lobby is a good option for the largest restroom location, but our preference is for a slightly offset restroom entry from the main lobby so that those entries have a degree of privacy while still being readily available.

- The ceiling in your lobby is a good place to do something interesting with a different material since it's front and center. Nicer materials can be used sparingly but powerfully in high-focus areas.

- Think about sound. The entry is likely to be your largest area of "uncontrolled" sound (the sanctuary will hold more people, but the environment is more controlled with regard to people talking or singing). You may need to consider at least some softer surfaces such as carpet, carpet tiles, or even some sound absorption panels on the walls.

- Consider designing the wall between the lobby and sanctuary as something that could possibly be propped open for overflow during a special situation (a large funeral or wedding, for example).

- Consider having some ceiling or wall-mounted TVs in this area for announcements or closed circuit delivery of the speaker's message.

- Ideally, a lobby will have at least two different "centers": a place for refreshments such as coffee or water, and a place to distribute information. It is not ideal (although certainly possible in a pinch) to have these two centers in the same place. Typically, these ministries are manned by several people who need some room, and spills are also a factor for the refreshment area. If you are considering solid-surface countertops, such as granite, anywhere in the building, this would be the one place to splurge because it is a high-traffic area.

- Handicapped spaces need to be as close to the entry doors as possible, with ramps as needed (your architect will figure this out!)
- Simple, low-water plants and shrubs carry their weight when it comes to welcoming elements. Do not get carried away on landscaping unless you have someone willing to maintain it over the long haul. It's better to do something simple and welcoming, which is likely to already be your building strategy. Look into **xeriscaping*** as a concept.

As a Rule of Thumb, you can figure on about two to three square feet of space for every seat in the sanctuary for your foyer/lobby. Foyers will be heavily used for purposes other than traffic flow. Some examples of additional uses include: overflow for sanctuary and/or fellowship, Bible study space, coffee bar traffic, information centers, places for conversations, and much more!

WORSHIP SPACES

What is your perception of the ideal worship space? Do you think metal chairs arranged skillfully on a basketball court make a great sanctuary, or are you visualizing a space with beautiful wooden pews and stained glass? The truth is that both scenarios work amazingly well. Your architect will ask to hear your general ideas, and you'll then want your architect to provide you with as many options as possible so that you know your alternatives.

> What is your perception of the ideal worship space?

---

* **xeriscaping**—landscaping that reduces or even eliminates the need for regular watering.

To begin, think about what your typical worship looks like. If your worship service greatly resembles a Hillsong concert, you will need to approach it differently than if your congregation sings a cappella. You will need more room per person if you are encouraging more freedom of expression during worship.

A good Rule of Thumb to figure the worship space is to use about 25 square feet per person. This formula includes the sanctuary and its direct support spaces: the baptistery, a dressing room, a bank of restrooms, and a foyer/lobby.

Here are some other items to consider as you contemplate the worship space:

- If your church needs a permanent baptistery installed, a pre-fab model is the best option, and it usually comes with an option to purchase a heater (a major plus).
- If you have a choir, you'll need to estimate a target number of participants and factor that number into your stage size.
- Enlist a person to itemize the sound and lighting equipment you currently own. Will you use all of this, move it to a new fellowship area eventually, or dedicate it for another use? Ask the person to make some general projections on each piece of equipment as to what the longer-term goals might be.
- Sound booths can be done well either as permanent or portable units, but they need a place where the person in the booth can hear very well. Most "sound people" will request a location in the dead center of the church, and some churches accommodate this by creating two aisles around the booth. Most opt to move the sound booth to the side slightly and keep a center aisle (mostly for the capability to have a center aisle during weddings!)
- An **acoustician** is a person who specializes in determining the very specific qualities a building needs for optimal sound. He looks at the space in terms of very specific music instruments, the angle of the walls, and the properties of materials such as brick or glass. An acoustician will take an architect's **3D model** and let you know exactly how you could tweak the sanctuary to create amazing sound.

FELLOWSHIP SPACES

Fellowship spaces differ greatly, but one thing is usually a constant: people like to eat and hang out! The fellowship area usually works to meet this need, in addition to other congregational ministry needs such as sports and other large group events. Here are some thoughts:

- Consider a location close to the kitchen for ease of serving
- You'll want to consider this room as high-traffic, because it likely will be! Carpet tiles, stained concrete, and vinyl tile are by far the best flooring options for fellowship areas depending on your specific uses (receptions, basketball games, etc.).
- If you are aiming for a truly multipurpose space, consider some dimmable lighting and a neutral color palette. With these choices, a basketball court can serve well for a wedding reception and other special occasions.
- If you are considering hosting basketball, volleyball, or other sports or games, you'll need a taller building than if the fellowship hall is strictly for eating purposes.
- If you are planning an opening between the kitchen and the fellowship area, metal overhead doors work well as dividers. If these are too much for your budget, consider using some shutters to separate the space.
- Take time to explain to your architect (or write a summary) of how your cooking/warming/serving process actually works. If you don't currently serve food because you don't have the facilities, you might talk to some churches who do it well and ask if you can participate sometime to get a feel for some good systems.
- If you can afford it, having dedicated storage for tablecloths, drink pitchers, and coffee dispensers when they're clean is a great amenity. Since they are food storage items, it's important that they stay clean.
- Sound will be a factor in a fellowship space. If you (for various reasons) cannot use a softer floor or ceiling material, you'll need to consider some acoustical panels.

- Plan for special presentations in this space by determining where you might place a portable stage and sound equipment, and definitely consider power and data requirements.
- Most churches plan to seat at least half of their worship attendance in the fellowship center. Small churches (under 200 attendees) are very likely to need to seat closer to their total worship attendance. Plan for 15 square feet per person for the fellowship center if you are going to use long rectangular tables or 18–20 square feet per person if you are planning for round tables. This includes the dining/fellowship room, the kitchen, and the restrooms.

CHILDREN'S SPACES

Children's areas don't have to be heavily decorated—they need to be clean and inviting. Many times the children's ministry warrants its own master planning exercise because there are so many involved ministries that depend on these facilities. For instance, is a Mother's Day Out (MDO) in your future? Do you have plans for a school one day? Are you going to allow other groups to use the children's wing, such as a home school group or co-op? If so, how are you going to meet these needs? Brainstorming sessions can help you define what the possibilities are. Here are some helpful hints involving children:

- You must think about the nature of children. They are easily distracted. They have a lot of energy. You want to help them focus, and you want them to get engaged, but not *too* excited. Aiming for "exciting with some structure" is a good goal!
- With that in mind, it's a great idea to focus on one or two elements per space that are special about that one space, so that children begin to identify with attending. For instance, creating a simple wayfinding system for the kids by making each room's door or entry mat a different color. It's another way of ministering to the smallest members of your church family by making them feel safe and comfortable.
- Most churches prefer the nursery to be located fairly near the sanctuary. Near the nursery, many churches are also adding a

lounge for mothers with newborns. When a woman has a newborn or any kind of special needs child, it is wonderful of a church to think of those needs. Having a small room with rocking chairs, some foot stools, a small sink, a place to change a diaper, and perhaps an under-counter fridge can often determine whether a family can make it to a service or not! These accommodations are very easy for the architect to plan for, and then the church can simply put together whatever furniture works best, as funds become available.

- Many churches offer a three to four-hour per week program to give moms and dads a little break. Keep in mind that activities such as Mother's Day Out programs have slightly different code requirements, such as requiring sinks in classrooms. If you do have dreams of doing a school or MDO one day, make sure you mention this to your architect so they can make sure you're set up for that. You don't have to build out every specific detail upfront, but planning is key here!

> Is a Mother's Day Out (MDO) in your future? Do you have plans for a school one day? Are you going to allow other groups to use the children's wing, such as a home school group or co-op? If so, how are you going to meet these needs?

CHILDREN'S SECURITY

We live in a different world than our parents did. Luckily, very simple and economical efforts can provide lots of safety for the kids!

It's common in mid- to large-sized churches for children to be checked in to class or childcare. Churches that are smaller or have had the same childcare programs for many years may have chosen not to tackle this initiative yet. Planning is key, though, and you need to think in terms of "phases" of child security. If you can't check them in using a computer system yet, you can start by at least documenting who is where on a clipboard. Start doing this, and it will become second nature in a few months. At some point, you will need a place where you can put a desk and check-in station. Consider data and electrical needs for that space, as a laptop and printer will likely be placed in that space. Once a child is checked in to the children's area, most parents believe they will not be let out until they are picked up, so ideally there needs to be a restroom inside that children's area. If that is not feasible, you'll need to create a policy for how children will be escorted safely to the restroom and back to the classrooms.

The children's area will also need to have proper fire egress (have your architect verify this for you).

STORAGE

Churches usually feel they don't have enough storage. Here are some helpful tips:

- Sunday School teachers need storage. A teacher cabinet per classroom is ideal, as are some cubbies and hooks for the children's belongings. Each teacher might keep a plastic tub in the cabinet with class-specific items, and then common items could be shared. Usually, only volunteers who are currently teaching get to keep their personal materials at the church.

- As a general rule of thumb, these items always need their own space: chairs and tables, banquet/fellowship items, janitorial items, server/data equipment (this room needs to stay cool 24/7!), seasonal decorations, books for pastoral research and church use, and communion supplies (these sometimes need to be stored in a refrigerator in close proximity to a sink area).

- Will non-church ministries using your space be allowed to store items? If so, where? Consider a common space for this should you allow it. For example, maybe AA meets at your building on Thursdays and would like to store some books. If that's okay with you, perhaps a dedicated space for all non-church users would be a good choice. When it fills up, you can politely ask the leaders to tidy up.

CHURCH RESTROOMS

The code requirement for church restrooms is rarely enough. A good indicator of what you need is the situation you currently have. Take some notes and let your architect know if there are long lines. Here are some considerations for the restrooms:

- 👍 A typical rule of thumb for the restroom requirement when it comes to worship spaces is to provide 1 fixture per 150 occupants in the men's room, and 1 fixture per 75 occupants for the women's room.
- 👍 In addition, you will generally need one sink/lavatory for 200 occupants. This rule of thumb is for both men and women.
- One handicapped stall is required in each restroom.
- If there are six stalls, there must also be an "ambulatory" stall, which means there will be grab bars for a person on crutches.
- Consider adding a family restroom for moms and dads (also appreciated by people with several children and single parents). The physically disabled will also appreciate family restrooms, as they are typically easier to navigate and offer increased privacy.

FOOD AND CLOTHING DISTRIBUTION CENTERS

Certainly, if you are running any type of food or clothing distribution center, you will need to discuss this project in detail with your architect because those types of ministries typically start small and grow at lightning speed. What may have initially fit into the context of whatever space it was allocated could soon need its own space.

- Take your architect on a personal tour of the distribution work you have going on. These stories are rarely communicated clearly through pictures and descriptions.
- Measurements and inventories are very important, as are numbers of volunteers and what their actual jobs are.

- We have never created more actual drawings for one room than for a "benevolence barn" that we drew very early in my career. These buildings work very hard! Remind your architect to consider every detail, including the weight capacities and depths of shelving.

OUTDOOR SPACES

Increasingly, churches are becoming intentional about designing their outdoor spaces for maximum use. Your architect should help you think about how you should orient the building so you can gain maximum shade for outdoor spaces.

> **Are there ministry opportunities, or even ongoing ministry efforts, that would be well-served by a functional outdoor space?**

- Consider working in a few semi-private areas outside, perhaps with half-walls, some landscaping, shade, and an outdoor fan.
- If at least some of your tasks can be completed outdoors (and the millennial work force loves to move around while working!), that change will free up some of your indoor space. This might not work June through September in Texas, but it would be a great amenity for the rest of the year.
- Possibilities for outdoor activities include lunch and break areas, conference spaces, and publicly open spaces.
- Here are some amenities that the church could offer outdoors to strangers and members alike: free WiFi, with a separate password for the porch areas, perhaps a switch for the outdoor fan, and a water fountain that fills up a bottle. Simple items like this will help welcome people to use the space even when you're not there.
- Are there ministry opportunities, or even ongoing ministry efforts, that would be well-served by a functional outdoor space?

WAYFINDING

Wayfinding addresses how a person navigates your facilities. Have you ever gone to an amusement park or someplace new and thought, "I do not know what I'm supposed to do. Where is the ticket counter? Are there strollers available? Is there even a clean restroom?"

Last year my husband and I took our boys to Legoland. Neither of us can stand amusement parks, so we were there only in support of a six-year-old's obsession with Legos. We walked up to the enormous entry, ready to watch our two angels like hawks for the next six hours as they would surely be darting around. Our stress levels were high.

To our surprise, the moment we cleared the giant arching sign, we felt as if someone had said,

"Hello, here's everything you could ever need today." There were signs clearly indicating clean restrooms within eyeshot and neatly arranged strollers available for refundable credit card or cash rental. They offered water, bottled for $2 or out of a fountain which filled your bottle (for free!) and a clean playground with benches for parents to sit, letting the children play while we waited without worry for the park to open. Clean, easy to read maps showed us which paths to take for younger children, versus another path designed specifically for older children. They provided a coffee bar, with all of the cream and sugar you could want, and they had planted trees to offer shade. And yes, smiling workers were buzzing around ready to start their day. Within five minutes, we looked at each other and came to silent agreement: today was not going to be terrible at all! We felt safe and comfortable, and we were not rushing to leave at all.

In fact, we had just walked into a brand new place, and *we could not wait to return.*

Thoughtfulness is incredibly important when designing your building. On our trip to Legoland, it felt like someone had designed the park just for us. Yet, I witnessed other people very different from ourselves experiencing the same feeling. At one point, I watched a military family in line that was greeted with a hefty discount and a sincere "thank you" from the woman working the counter.

Think through the different types of people who will come to your church. Start by dividing them into large and small categories for the sake of discussion. You should have a good number of categories to consider. There are couples, singles, parents, children who are walked in, children who walk around on their own, elderly people, handicapped people, teenagers, girls, boys, babies with special needs, parents with small children, and parents of school age children. Your church may have high school baseball players who don't attend during spring, grandparents who parent, moms who do and don't have husbands, single dads, seventh graders with eating disorders, children with good home lives, and thirty-year-olds with baggage. You could have alcoholics who are in rehab, sex offenders, rich people with issues, people whose parents drop them off, people who are picked up in a van, and moms with newborn babies. The larger the church, the longer and more diverse the list.

Was that list exhausting? Yes. Exhaustive? Not by a long shot.

Here's the point: each of these groups experiences your facility, and your church, differently. We can't control every individual's experience, but we can consider how we *want* them to experience coming to church. This conversation is not about your core twenty families. Those troopers would meet you in a ditch next Sunday if you asked them to, on time and with donuts and portable coffee in tow. Rather, this section is about ministering to the specific needs of the entire congregation.

For instance, consider a new mom. Even if she has attended for years, she is going to need to figure out what life at church now looks like. Will I drop my baby off? How do I know he is safe? Where can I come back, feed the baby, and still get back to my Bible study quickly without missing much? How can your facility help her during the transition?

Small children are a group who will need consideration. Most churches like the idea of having small children (at least through preschool) located close to the sanctuary. It's helpful to have a room for new moms close to the sanctuary, and you may consider having closed-circuit television in the room. Classrooms or spaces for school-aged kids and youth can be located through a corridor, or in a separate building, provided there is clear and consistent signage from all entry locations.

Elderly and disabled people experience new places completely differently than the physically unchallenged. Because even small tasks can prove quite cumbersome, a simple, straightforward environment, which is well thought out and considerate is such a welcome, beautiful blessing to a person who is physically challenged. One church provided a single-stall family restroom nearest the sanctuary for the sole consideration of two members in wheelchairs who struggled with the long path to the restrooms. These restrooms were going in the building regardless, but the church's individual needs played a role in the specific location.

> We can't control every individual's experience, but we can consider how we want them to experience coming to church.

As another example, say there's something going on after church for a large group of people. How do you want that group to assimilate into the large area? The people serving the function need to have an alternative route so they can get over there faster and prepare, and you'll want the crowd to go the way that you want them to. These are all very specific instances where wayfinding is important.

> What should a brand new family's experience be? How can you set up your volunteers and staff to welcome them, and what clear signs do you need to have in place to make sure they can avoid confusion?

And then there's the brand new, intimidated family that hasn't darkened the door of a church building for ten years. What should a brand new family's experience be? How can you set up your volunteers and staff to welcome them, and what clear signs do you need to have in place to make sure they can avoid confusion? People can feel embarrassed if they're in a new environment and wandering around, trying to figure out where to go. Make sure the building is set up well to avoid discomfort and awkwardness.

How is your church demonstrating thoughtfulness to a diverse group of people (such as the list above)?

SAFETY AND SECURITY FOR THE BUILDING

Of course, most leaders know they need to secure their facilities. Here are specific items that will help you to be successful:

- Clearly, the church building will be open to anyone who needs you during working hours. You may even choose to post an after-hours number on the door should someone need you later on. But when the staff is gone, the building should be locked.
- Think about how you want your staff and ministry teams to get into the building. Limit the number of building keys you give out (I suggest the pastor, elders, and possibly the person in charge of the long-range facility plan have a key). Keys you do give out should be clearly marked "do not copy."
- Magnetic locks, code access, and card swipes are all good options for the remainder of the people needing building access. These can easily be manipulated as needed (by changing the code or disabling a card).
- Entry points need to be kept to a minimum without restricting traffic flow. There will be multiple exterior doors, mainly needed for fire exits, but you will want to restrict the use of those as entrances.
- When you are not there, the church needs to be well lit. Basic security lighting around the perimeter of the building is necessary, in addition to pole lighting in the parking lot.

PLACEMAKING

Placemaking is the concept of using shared amenities to increase social relationships by creating some strong ties to the identity of the place. Placemaking embodies being intentional with your efforts. For instance, a plaza shared by several buildings where workers sit down to rest and relax, have lunch, and experience the benefits created by the plaza. The end result is a strengthened relationship between people because of their shared interest in the plaza. Instead of just saying, "we need a building," we begin to realize small decisions are important because they can impact when people come and how long they will stay.

Contrary to what some may assume, expensive building materials rarely contribute to this phenomena. Of course, physical comfort plays a huge role. Proportions also play a large role in how comfortable we feel, as do colors and the availability of natural light. As we become more detailed in the descriptions of the spaces needed on our list, we can begin to consider traits that would make up the best spaces for each of our uses.

For example, heights of ceilings are a necessary discussion. When you get more than twenty or so people in a room, and you have a ceiling that's eight feet tall, it becomes very claustrophobic. Therefore, the larger the room and the more people likely to occupy it, the taller the ceilings need to be. This is one simple example, but we will want to look at each place/use and determine what characteristics would make it ideal for all of your uses. Later, we will need to prioritize, and some of these items may have to go or be postponed for a later phase; however, if we know what they are, we can plan ahead.

> **Keep yourself inspired along the way by visiting other churches and buildings you admire. Remember to have fun. Being a leader in this role is a great honor.**

Designing your building should be fun. Creating a space to host the needs of the entire ministry effort of the church, from worship and fellowship to everything that makes up your own church culture, may seem like a daunting task on some days—but on other days it will prove one of the most rewarding works of your life. Draw on your architect's team for their ideas and experience, but keep your eyes wide open for clever designs you can share with the group. Keep yourself inspired along the way by visiting other churches and buildings you admire. Remember to have fun. Being a leader in this role is a great honor.

Action Items:

1. Make sure that your research is complete (resources available at www.churchbuildingguide.com) so that you'll be able to strike when opportunity arises:

    a. Complete your Church Vision Plan
    b. Complete your Church Needs and Usage List
    c. Complete your Church Building Chronicle

    Do not wait until the subject comes up to complete your research and documentation. Once the "subject comes up," you will need to grab that info so that you can act.

2. Discuss names of representatives from the individual ministries of the church who could possibly consult upon request as related to very specific concerns in those spaces. Clear these names with the Elders or Pastor.

3. Set up some opportunities for the team to visit 2–3 churches with facilities you admire. Take pictures and document how the facilities relate to you own vision and culture.

    Ideas for Places to Visit:

    _____

    _____

    _____

    _____

    _____

Discussion Topics:

1. Have you ever noticed that in certain places, you are just apt to stay longer? What are some of those places, and what are the reasons you'll stay? How do you feel when you are there? Share with the group and discuss.

a. Place: _____

Characteristics: _____

When I'm there I feel: _____

b. Place: _____

Characteristics: _____

When I'm there I feel: _____

2. What traits make up your "ideal" worship space? Is this because it relates strongly to the culture of your church, or some other reason?

    _____

    _____

3. Are there ministry opportunities, or even ongoing ministry efforts, which would be served by functional outdoor spaces on your church site? Could these efforts easily be accomplished at a public park or other free space, or is there value in such spaces being located onsite? Is this value enough to warrant an investment in such elements?

4. Is there a specific group of people that your church would like to minister to as a church body? How can you design facilities to meet their needs?

    _____

    _____

If you are in a place where you would like to serve a group of people and do not quite know how, ask some members of that group to come talk to you about their needs. Really listen to what they tell you, and then visualize how you can possibly work to serve them and meet their real needs. What implications are there for your facilities?

5. What does your church culture indicate about when your church building needs to be open and available? What are some strategies for being available and helpful (even in off hours) that your church could implement?

_____

_____

Recap: *The built environment affects how we do life. Design decisions are far-reaching. The vision of the church needs to be the focus at all times so that you can work to create experiences that support the church's mission. Work to establish which portions of the project are needs and wants. Remember that everything can be phased—it does not need to happen overnight. Be strategic. Remember to have fun.*

Chapter 5

BUILDING YOUR BIGGEST MINISTRY TOOL

B y this point, you're probably getting a good feel for the times when you'll engage others to help you in planning and designing the facilities for your vision. Architects with experience, however, also rely heavily on the insight of other experts—namely, the construction manager who will be working with them on the project. One critical area where projects can go wrong is the failure to seek real-life knowledge of systems, strategic methods to meet budgets, and market conditions. It is imperative that you, your architect, and your construction manager work together so that you can consistently determine the best course of action for the church.

Here's a pretty common scenario when it comes to churches and building:

Let's say you find a piece of property, and through much hard work, research, and fundraising, you buy it. For the next year, you spend your time hunting down all the free help you can muster to put together a floor plan, a beautiful drawing, and some cost information for your dream. You present it to the church, and the elders decide to move forward. So far, besides the land, you have spent virtually nothing, and finally, after a year and a half, you have raised enough money to hire an architect to draw up the plans for your vision. Literally all you need is a professionally sealed plan. You diligently interview and then hire the best-suited team for the job.

Your new architect's team returns a month later, and after much study, there is news to report. The city is requiring more detention than you could ever have imagined. Code requirements for parking are ridiculous, in your opinion, but apparently necessary. The air conditioning tonnage required by the commercial energy code is blowing your mind. The final straw is that the building has to have a fire sprinkler system installed, which will likely cost you over a hundred thousand dollars. An easement at the back of the property is now driving design decisions, and there are constraints to deal with in every direction. You are, even if you are not admitting it, on the verge of a full panic. But faced with the truth, you move forward because, frankly, that seems to be the only option. You instruct the architect to make these changes, and in the process, you start to actually trust them. At least you are finally getting a clear picture. In a few months, you have everything you need to bid the job. You report the situation to the church and share your struggles, but promise that the realization of the vision is just ahead.

And so the architect puts the job out to bid. You wait three weeks. The architect answers questions. You show up cautiously in a group to consider each bidder's qualifications and price.

But the bottom falls out. You are fifty percent over budget. Anxiously, you search your options. Maybe the bank would lend a bit more, but you're not 100% sure that's even responsible. Clearly, you will go back to the congregation for more, but the dread starts to set in. You go down the list and think of each of your members and what they have given, some even sacrificially, and you're fairly convinced that the well has almost run dry. Faced with what seems like a hopeless situation, you begin the conversation of what parts of the building can be cut to get into budget. With every cut, you start to realize the disappointment coming for the congregation (and you).

There is no way to camouflage your frustration, and you begin to explain this to your architect. Maybe they drew some things that were too fancy and expensive for your church. These are easy enough to remove, but that's just not enough. More than that, you are overwhelmingly frustrated by the contractor's assessment of the price. He is saying prices have gone *up, especially since you started the project two years ago. On some level, you know he is telling you the truth. But the question remains: how did you not see this coming?*

How did you not see this coming?

Well, churches are doing ministry-related things. While business owners, school districts, and large companies are by their very nature immersed in the cost of these industries, churches are not. Churches are gathering food, helping the hurting, and working to reach people spiritually. Until you embark on a building project for yourself, it's quite possible you have zero information on the subject on a regular basis.

Churches, and their leadership teams in particular, need help planning and budgeting the facilities which will serve as their single largest and most influential ministry tool.

Planning is the key that most churches either forget or neglect— or even worse, push through on limited or unqualified advice. Your most critical planning needs arise, ironically, right at the onset of your vision, when you can least afford them. Resist the urge to use budgeting challenges as an excuse to neglect seeking help and good advice. You can find a team who will partner with you—and with each other—in a long-term, mutually satisfying relationship that benefits your church.

> **Your most critical planning needs arise, ironically, right at the onset of your vision, when you can least afford them.**

From the very beginning of designing a project, every church needs to prayerfully consider partnering with a qualified construction professional who can offer their skills and expertise to benefit the church. Putting the construction part of your team into reactionary mode (for instance, asking them to tell you the budget after you've worked for six months to design a building) is heading straight for disappointment. So, what are the right questions to ask a construction professional, and how does "that side" work? What do they bring to the table, and how do you make the most of this relationship? In this chapter, we'll discuss the answers to these questions.

While it is easy to think that construction managers don't need to be involved until later in the building process, they actually need to get involved at the same time the architect is involved, or very shortly thereafter. Here are the most critical areas where we need construction managers engaged as the planning stages are getting underway:

- Market conditions change rapidly in today's economy, so we need to get an update on current prices routinely.
- In light of the size and needs of the church, the construction manager can tell us what type of structural system (e.g., wood-framed, pre-engineered metal building, or structural steel) is most cost-effective for the project.
- The construction manager can give market-accurate input on how to design the mechanical systems to ensure the best value for the church (a big-ticket cost item).
- The construction manager's ability to visit and consult onsite is *extremely valuable*. Once construction specialists lay their eyes on the chosen site, they can tell us if any items are jumping out as highly challenging or likely to drive up the price. In new construction projects, this is my highest recommendation. On renovations, it's an absolute must.
- Construction managers, due to their knowledge of building system integration (like how the structural system meets the mechanical system, etc.), have a keen sense for recommending very cost-effective phasing opportunities. I always want to hear their best recommendation for phasing a campus or series of projects over time, as well as designing to accommodate future expansions with minimal waste.
- And finally, the most important role that your construction manager will fill from day one is figuring out how much construction you specifically can afford with your budget.

Of course, your construction manager will be involved throughout much more than just the beginning stages. As the building project progresses, your contractor will progressively become more heavily involved. The remaining sections will discuss how to navigate your relationship with your contractor as well as the essential tips you'll need throughout construction planning.

PROJECT BUDGETS

The time to set the project budget is right around the beginning of design work, and that decision needs to be made in close counsel with a *team* of people who have multiple examples of recent, similar projects in the same geographical area. After the initial project budget is set for the church, it needs to be re-evaluated alongside each subsequent milestone. If a portion of the project is affecting the budget more than it should (e.g., square footage, building systems such as structural or mechanical, and finish choices), the church leadership team needs to know as quickly as possible so that they can decide the best course of action.

> **After the initial project budget is set for the church, it needs to be re-evaluated alongside each subsequent milestone.**

Architects who design with no knowledge of the budget are often accused of "designing in a vacuum." This arrangement typically creates large-scale disappointment for the congregation. Of course, the architect will need to work toward the budget the church designates for the new building project, and there will likely be points where the pastor needs to approach the church for additional funds. However, the problem occurs when a church is working fervently to raise $1,000,000, only to find out three years later that they need three times that amount to accomplish the plan they had decided on. Regardless of what you may perceive, architects do not have first-hand, daily access to construction costs. There is another partner needed for this, and that is the construction manager.

IS THERE A MAGIC FORMULA FOR BUDGETING CONSTRUCTION?

While there is no precise magic formula, one formula is useful. The very best thing a church can do as they predict their budget is to:

- Know their story (most do)
- Understand where they stand with regard to what they have and what they need (some do)
- Balance their needs and wants with their financial means (most do not, at least at first).

Here is a simple formula to help create clarity in your mind. (Grab the full-color diagram online at www.churchbuildingguide.com for help in illustrating this principle):

Consider that a project (let's just say a building) comprises a triangular, balanced relationship of three variables: **budget** (the available funds), **scope** (the size or square footage of the project), and **quality** (the specific choices about products, land, building type, etc.). Each of these elements takes up one point on the triangle. When balanced properly, the project is on budget, is the correct size, and is pleasing to the church in terms of functionality and design. Now, pretend this scenario is you, and it may or may not have a familiar ring to it:

I have the potential to raise and borrow a total of $1,000,000. I need 6,500 square feet of new building space according to the dimensions I took of my current facilities and the free advice of industry professionals in the congregation. I would like a metal building with some nicer finishes on the front and some parking.

Let's begin by placing each of these "needs" on the triangle.

- Budget = $1,000,000
- Scope = 6,500 square feet
- Quality = "metal building"

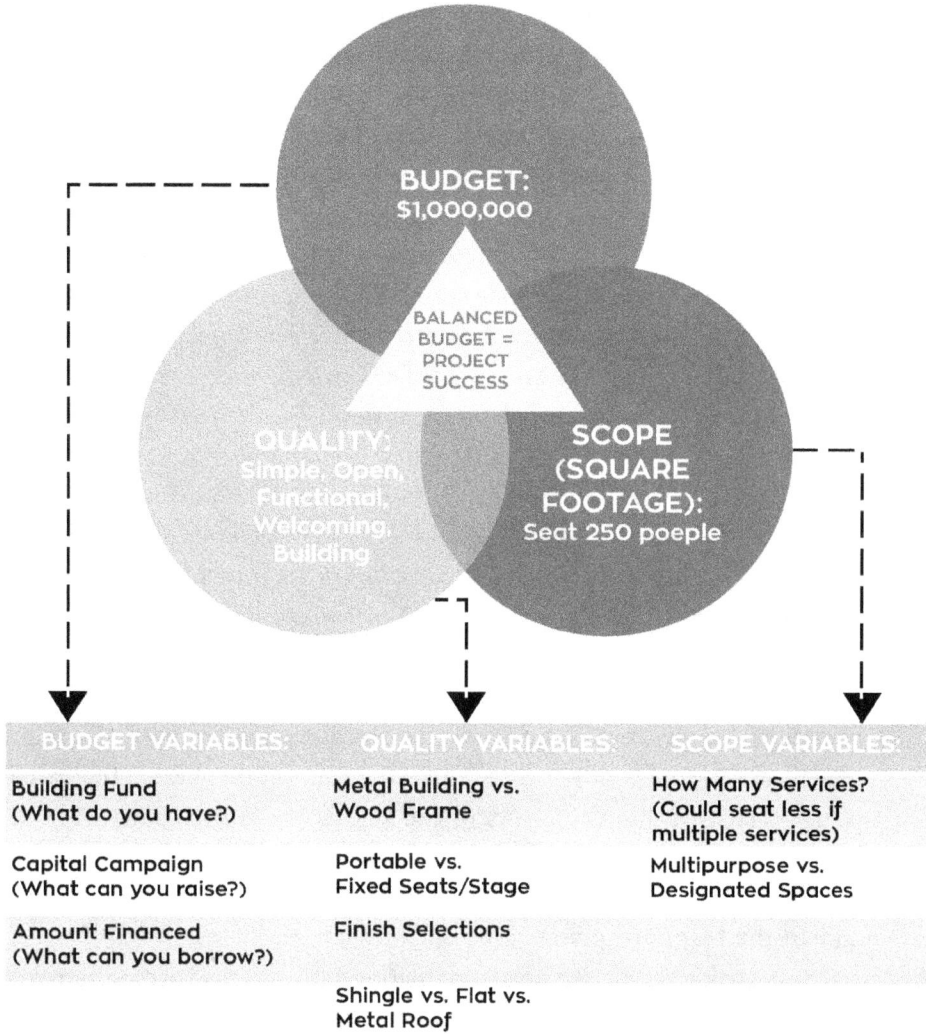

BUDGET:
$1,000,000

BALANCED BUDGET = PROJECT SUCCESS

QUALITY:
Simple, Open, Functional, Welcoming, Building

SCOPE (SQUARE FOOTAGE):
Seat 250 poeple

BUDGET VARIABLES:	QUALITY VARIABLES:	SCOPE VARIABLES:
Building Fund (What do you have?)	Metal Building vs. Wood Frame	How Many Services? (Could seat less if multiple services)
Capital Campaign (What can you raise?)	Portable vs. Fixed Seats/Stage	Multipurpose vs. Designated Spaces
Amount Financed (What can you borrow?)	Finish Selections	
	Shingle vs. Flat vs. Metal Roof	

PROJECT BUDGET BALANCER
SCOPE QUALITY BUDGET

Here's a tip. Consider each point on the triangle and decide which one is the non-negotiable, must-have priority. Let's say in this case the $1,000,000 **budget** is the priority—you cannot borrow more money, the well is tapped dry, and you have no building fund. So that's your fixed variable. The **scope** is 6,500 square feet. We do some investigating and find out that everyone's considering a sanctuary for 250 people. Our question now is, could you have two services and build a smaller sanctuary? Could you have three services? As for the **quality**, could you possibly move from a metal building to a more economical wood-frame building? Could you use a simpler roof system?

The point is to figure out the negotiables and the fixed variables and then discuss them. Most end up deciding that if they can adjust all three categories (raise a little more money, build a little less, and save just a couple items for a later phase), the budget ends up balancing out. *If you are able to give your team of professionals some freedom to suggest ideas on at least two of the variables in the triangle, a good team should always be able to solve your puzzle.* If you are holding tightly to all variables, you have placed your team in a place where they will not be able to help you. Assuming you trust your team, you will come to realize that they do not control the construction market or the price of materials, nor do they control the size of the room that will hold your congregation. If you're at the point where your equation needs to be balanced, loosen the reigns just slightly on two of your variables and let the team bring you some options.

Some will scratch their heads on this one, but a church is a **commercial building** subject to state requirements for **fire safety accessibility, parking requirements, plumbing fixture count requirements, fresh air requirements, building envelope requirements, water detention,** and so on. The reason for this is largely that churches are places where large groups of people congregate. When dealing with the health, safety, and welfare of the public, the state imposes regulations. Your new guest on Sunday doesn't think anything of walking into your building—they assume it's safe, and it should be. If they happen to be in a wheelchair, they have a right to be able to enter the facility with as much ease as possible.

In every situation, **commercial buildings*** have requirements that homes do not, and they cost more. Consider what your house might cost per square foot if you added all of these items, and the price may make more sense.

WHAT CAN WE DO TO SAVE MONEY?

The first thing you can do to save money is hire a qualified construction professional for simple, reasonably priced services that benefit the church at the very beginning of the project. Not every company offers these types of pre-construction services, but you *can* find a company who does. Having information you can rely on from a qualified contractor is critical to project success. You do not need to commit to building the project or sign a complicated contract. What you need is someone who can advise you throughout the process, and you should compensate them for those services accordingly. (During design, you'll notice that largely the architect is managing the overall project, while the contractor plays a support role. During construction, the opposite is true.)

Before you ever ask a construction professional to quote you numbers, give him a chance to hear in full what you want to do. It astounds me that church leaders will often spend hours with my architectural team discussing very specific needs and then ask the contractor within five minutes of an introduction how much their building will cost. Typically, this question is phrased more like, "What's a 10,000 square foot building running these days?" The truth is that he has *no idea* how much your building will cost. He has no idea what you are going to put into your building, and he probably has no clue what your site conditions are. On every level, this is a completely irrelevant question. If you are asking about a renovation, multiply that irrelevance by 10.

---

* **commercial building**—as related to church construction, a commercial building is a building which is not residential in nature and is therefore subject to local, state, and federal codes.

Before you ever ask anyone to quote you numbers, give him a chance to hear in full what you want to do.

The contractor likely has customers who are paying more because they have specific needs, and some who are paying less because they have a perfect site in the middle of nowhere where there is no city jurisdiction in charge. Understand that *you are asking a loaded question*, and he will need to know more information before giving you accurate information.

The right way to approach pricing your job is to have the contractor present in the early discussions so he has a clear understanding of your goals. When the architect draws up something you like, let the contractor look at the ideas. Let him go out to the site. In fact, ask him to go out there whenever he wants. Give him time to ask questions. Give the architect (and your team) time to respond. You need to give the contractor some time to do a basic cost estimation, and then you need to meet with him so that he can present his thoughts about your project. At this stage of the game, final design decisions have not been made, so there is a lot of guesswork.

Very likely, the first time you see the estimated number for your project, you will want to fall out of your chair.

Many church leaders become nervous at this point, immediately wondering if they have messed up. You haven't messed up. You're making your wish list. There's nothing wrong with communicating honestly about what you like and what you need, but now you know your **parameters*** and can approach the rest of the design phase, budget triangle in hand, with more reasonable expectations.

If you need to update the congregation because you've previously told them you would build something you no longer believe to be possible, communicate honestly. You will gain their respect and trust in the long run.

---

* parameters—guidelines which create a reasonable area for successfully accomplishing work (Ex: an architect might say, "We are waiting for the contractor to offer some budget parameters for that part of the project before we choose the finishes.")

BUILDING COST VERSUS PROJECT COST

When you receive general cost information from your construction professionals, understand that you'll need to think in terms of **project cost**, not just **building cost**. The building cost is the cost of the physical building itself: the walls and systems such as the slab, the roof, and the air conditioning, etc. The project cost is the total cost of the entire effort.

If, during an early discussion, the contractor says, "You're looking at about *x* dollars per square foot," he is talking about only the cost of the building and most likely the cost of his services to build it (be sure to confirm). He is saying that if you build a 5,000 square foot structure that *structure itself* will cost you 5,000 times *x*. He is not referring to the cost of the project, which would include the fees for the architect, the landscaping, the furniture and sound equipment, and the many other items that typically go into the cost of such a project. Your architect or contractor should be able to provide you with such a list early on to avoid confusion and forgetting critical cost elements.

What are some items you will need to factor into your project cost? Some of the items recommended by Texas Baptists are the building permit, testing fees, accessibility reviews and inspections, design fees, etc.

> **What are some items you will need to factor into your project cost?**

As a good Rule of Thumb, both Texas Baptists and our own company recommend reserving at least 15% of **contingency** when budgeting. Contingency is a word to describe reserve funds for unforeseen conditions.

This group is an excellent resource for fact-finding—be sure to visit them at www.texasbaptists.org.

DURING DESIGN

During design, the contractor ideally functions in a supportive role to the architect who is managing the project throughout that phase. What does this relationship look like? The contractor answers questions about the design, helps simplify complicated situations into cost-friendly solutions, and routinely provides cost updates as changes are made to the drawings. There is a back-and-forth nature to this stage, in that each time progress is made on the drawings, they need to be forwarded to the contractor for cost evaluation. Do not be surprised by the healthy conflict between the architect and contractor likely to arise during this phase as cost analyses are provided in response to the drawings. It is better to have these conversations now while the project exists on paper!

It is imperative that some conflict occur at this stage of the game. I'll explain. Let's say you're a little over budget in the beginning phases (this will always happen for a church).

Do you know what happens when the "price" is a bit too high during design? *The team has to work harder, which leads to innovation.* Those are the ingredients of a unique, functional space of greatest value to a church body. If you're totally out of the ballpark, that's one thing. In most cases, though, the design phase is just the place to work as hard as you can until the budget triangle balances itself out.

HVAC SYSTEMS AND WHY THEY MATTER

HVAC stands for Heating, Ventilating, and Air Conditioning, and when it comes to cost, these systems matter in a big way. There are many types of systems, ranging in cost from the type you would put in your house (which are generally more expensive to run), to high-performance chilled water systems that are put in schools or hospitals.

Your needs will most likely be somewhere in the middle, and you also need to consider what your operating costs are going to be. Fresh air requirements and **building envelope*** requirements are going to play a major role here. **Energy codes*** require a certain level of **building**

---

* **building envelope requirements**—code requirements telling you the amount and type of materials which are allowed as part of your exterior walls and roof systems in order to meet code.

* **energy codes**—minimum requirements for energy efficiency in building design and construction.

* **building performance**—a description of a building's energy efficiency, typically based on the mechanical systems and building envelope properties.

performance* in commercial construction with respect to items such as lighting, mechanical equipment, electrical elements, plumbing, and your building envelope.

These mechanical system requirements will always be more than you prefer to build and yield costs more than you expect to pay. On the upside, operating costs for buildings meeting energy code are significantly less.

YOUR STRUCTURAL SYSTEMS

What we need the contractor's input on here is what structural members should actually hold your building up, in very specific terms. We then need information on market conditions of steel and wood, as well as their overall opinion of the situation at hand, because that is very valuable in terms of cost. Let's say I design an entire building in steel, but then on bid day I am told that wood would have saved a great deal of money. Can I ask the contractor to have a framing subcontractor price the building structure in wood? Sure, and he probably will oblige. However, there are two big problems here. One, we will not see the same type of competition between subcontractors on that portion of the work because the drawings are showing steel—it's very likely that the project isn't even on their radar. And two, the entire drawing set is designed around a critical element which is now gone. This has the makings of a nightmare during construction. So it is very important to ask the contractor's recommendation upfront and then make that recommendation a big part of the discussion early on. Big savings are at stake.

PRE-ENGINEERED METAL BUILDINGS (PEMB)

When people say "metal building," they are usually describing a building that has metal on the outside and on the roof. In the construction industry, however, the term **"metal building"*** refers to the building's

---

* **metal building**—a structural system, composed of pre-engineered metal members

structural* system. A metal building, to an architect or contractor, is a **pre-engineered metal building**. Pre-engineered metal buildings are wonderful for several reasons. They offer the possibility of large, open spans without columns, and they are generally very cost-friendly. Engineering for PEMBs takes place within the company that manufactures them (the manufacturer seals the drawings during the shop drawing process). However, the columns are large and often angled (although you can certainly specify straight columns for a PEMB). Without significant effort during design, the columns are likely to be located in unfortunate places (such as in a restroom where ADA clearances are needed). There is much coordination required by a professional architect and structural engineer, but these systems are a great option!

WOOD-FRAMED STRUCTURES

Smaller church buildings can be well-served by **wood-framed buildings** (this is the way houses are typically built). Wood-framed buildings are the most economical, and they provide a little more flexibility as far as the actual dimensions of each room (whereas with PEMBs, the column locations are fixed). The challenge with a wood-framed building is when you need too large of a span in one space (such as a sanctuary). **Glulam** systems are also good options for wood construction, depending on the circumstances.

STRUCTURAL STEEL

Structural steel offers an enormous range of flexibility and possibilities, and for that reason the system comes at a higher price than other systems. However, depending on the cost of steel and fuel and the overall design of the building, many times it is a viable option for certain portions of a building. In tight spaces where mechanical equipment needs to be stored on the roof, structural steel can work well. In addition, there are almost no design constraints, as individual members are much smaller than in a PEMB.

---

* **structural**—Any trade, occupation, or term related to the building's ability to stand up to and carry loads (wind loads, roof loads, etc.).

PERMITTING

Around the time your job goes to bid, you, your contractor, and your architect will need to attend a meeting with the city to discuss the project and begin the permitting process. Pulling the permit is a shared responsibility because technically the owner (the church) bears responsibility, but churches need help navigating the permit process. Typically, the architect is responsible for making sure the drawings meet code, an area that the city will evaluate heavily during the permitting process. It is a huge advantage, however, to have a contractor with experience getting initiatives pushed through and generally not being "hung up" in the red tape that municipalities are famous for. Such an experience can really break the church's fundraising effort should things be hung up for long periods.

DURING CONSTRUCTION: MEETINGS AND COMMUNICATION

Few days are more exciting in the church building process than the day the first piece of equipment arrives on-site! Once your project is officially under construction, you will see an immediate shift in lines of communication. The beginning of construction is a major milestone, and at that point, your architect will shift from a management role into a support role. For all practical purposes from that point forward, you will be in more contact with the contractor, and you will see the architect's team (usually not your designing architect, but a person skilled in construction administration) at monthly meetings. The contractor should explain to you who your main point of contact with the company will be. Likely, that will be a Project Manager. From the church's standpoint, the Building Committee Chair would be the construction company's first point of contact (and truly the only person who should call them for construction-related conversations).

Those two people can then communicate information to their respective groups efficiently and without confusion.

Usually, the architect, contractor, and building committee or committee chair meet on-site (or nearby) monthly during construction. The contractor is charged with running the meetings and will tell the group about the progress, any questions that have arisen, and a small forecast of what's ahead. (Right after this meeting is a great time for a congregational update!) Once the building is up and things are moving inside, a building tour is usually part of the monthly meeting.

Sometimes, the discussion can turn to construction lingo between the professionals, and at times, the church team can feel confused about the issue at hand. If this situation happens, immediately ask for clarification. Do not confirm agreement on issues until you fully understand what's going on. Construction people love to talk construction, and they don't think you're stupid for not understanding. Just about everyone on the project team learns something new every day. A simple, "Hey, back up. What's going on?" will enable you to move forward with confidence. Keep the communication open!

In addition, at these meetings you will discuss compensation for the contractor. Prior to the meeting, the contractor will have done an assessment of the work completed on site and completed an **Application for Payment***. This document is then submitted to the architect, who surveys the job to confirm agreement of the work to be completed and signs accordingly (or forwards his comments over, should he disagree). Once the architect signs, the church owes the contractor for the amount stipulated. If your available funds are partially a bank loan, you will need to advise the loan officer of when to expect these **Pay Apps**, or Applications for Payment. Be sure to ask what the terms for payment are so that you can consistently pay on time (and thereby make sure that all the subcontractors and workers on your job are able to be paid on time as well).

SAFETY

Safety on a construction site is of utmost importance. You need to ask your construction company to explain the specific details of their safety program, but here are some basic guidelines for all jobsites:

- Check in with the project superintendent when you come on-site. He will tell you which areas are safe and accompany you for a walk-through if you desire.

---

* **Application for Payment (Pay App)**—the contractor's typical method of invoice for payment. It provides a method of documenting what items and materials have been provided as well as tracking the current cost of the job.

- If your group would like a building tour on a day other than a scheduled meeting, you should call the construction company and offer some notice so that they can prepare to make the building safe during that time.
- Your contractor should be taking layers upon layers of expensive and time-consuming precautions to avoid injury. If church members enter the building without asking or checking in, exposing themselves to danger, their behavior is considered extremely disrespectful. If this happens repeatedly, you can expect changes in your relationship with the construction company because some trust has been broken. (Even as the **Architect of Record***, I would never enter a building without first checking in with the job superintendent. This rule goes for everyone.)
- *It is your responsibility to communicate the rules of the jobsite to the congregation.*
- At important milestones, the pastor may like to take the congregation on an in-progress tour! Scheduled ahead of time, this is a great experience for everyone involved and an amazing fundraising opportunity mid-construction. Activities such as praying over rooms and creating boards of encouragement for the workers are always wonderful moments in the journey.

"Construction" can be a polarizing word. For every person who has had a great experience building a building, there is one (or more) who has had a rough time. So, here is a little analogy for fun. If the planning phase is comparable to the excited stress of being a newlywed, and if the design phase is comparable to the exhaustive joy of a small child, undoubtedly the construction phase is something like having a teenager. With careful planning, good decisions, and guidance during design, the construction phase can be a rewarding and hopeful time made up of less work on the part of the church leadership. An overall excitement for the congregation will surely follow, as they start to see their future place of worship come to life. On the flip side—you get it.

---

* **Architect of Record**—the individual whose license/seal appears on a set of construction documents. This person is usually the owner or a principal in an architectural firm.

Construction can be a nightmare for those who fail to handle the design phase prudently and seriously. Plan early and often, and always with the end result (the vision) in mind.

Action Items:

1. Make a list of the top 4 planning tasks discussed so far that would benefit your church's ability to visualize the future facilities:

    a. _____

    _____

    b. _____

    _____

    c. _____

    _____

    d. _____

    _____

2. Print and discuss the illustration for the Budget Scope Quality triangle as a group. What is your main takeaway for your church from this illustration?

3. If you are in the midst of your own budget troubleshoot (actually, on really any issue!), print out a blank copy of the Budget Scope Quality triangle at www.churchbuildingguide.com. Try to merge your conversation with the concept of balancing these elements.

4. Visit Texas Baptists at www.texasbaptists.org for a good list of elements that make up the project cost versus the building cost. Start your own list of items that will be factors in your project one day, and keep that list filed for easy access.

Discussion Topics:

1. How will the way that your building is used possibly influence the design of systems such as the mechanical system? What spaces would benefit the culture of the church to be available during the week, and which ones can be used on occasion throughout the week?

   _____

   _____

2. How can your building committee portray a realistic picture of the church in the way that you respond to your contractor's commitment to safety?

   _____

   _____

3. What does your church culture say about resolving problems? Construction, in the best of scenarios and by its very nature, is a process made up of challenges built on other challenges. Many are unforeseen to all, and unexpected by the committee. What will your philosophy be when this occurs?

   _____

   _____

Recap: *In almost all cases, the investment in your church's facilities is the single largest expense your church will endure in its lifetime, and for good reason. These spaces are your largest working ministry tool! In all practicality, a church needs access to the input of a construction professional throughout the life of the church.*

Chapter 6

FINDING AND WORKING WITH YOUR PARTNERS

"How do we decide who to hire?" is a question that can baffle and divide people, as building committee members only want to make the "right" choice when it comes to bringing in professionals. These professionals will be charged with the complicated tasks of designing and constructing the church's facilities. These are people whom the church will have to trust to act in their best interest for years on end, and in most cases, they are usually just strangers at first.

It's important here that I tell you about when the wheels began to turn in our minds about how church projects really ought to be designed and built. Very early on, PlanNorth had just completed three successful projects where we got drawings out the door efficiently, and the churches loved the design work. As construction took off on these, we swallowed our pride and relied heavily on a seasoned construction manager to coach us through means and methods as we focused on codes and details. The buildings opened on time—gorgeous and as perfect as new buildings can possibly be. Since our firm was still new, I was incredibly grateful for the success of the projects, and I was ready to regroup for a bit.

When the prospect for designing an 800-seat sanctuary came up merely weeks later, my first thought was to pass on the project. The project was more than twice the physical size of our largest design project to date. My team, which now included two people with over 30 years' experience each (no accident there, I assure you), promised me that we were qualified. I should go to the meeting, they said, and assure the church we could do the project.

I went with the construction manager to the first meeting with the church, taking a little book of the other churches we'd done. As we walked in, the five smiling faces looking back at us were full of hope. Clearly, they had waited a long time for this. Excitedly, they told us their plans for growth. They told us their budget and how they were actively raising more. They told us about the 600 or so people involved who were donating sacrificially and of all of their prior construction phases, one of which was the building we were meeting in. It had been a rough experience, they told us openly, sparing the details but communicating that time and funds had been lost through a careless contractor and overzealous architect. They told of their children's ministry, their music ministry, their weekly events and the make-shift way they were making room for all of it. The construction manager, who had a good relationship with the group already, shared very helpful advice, and then much too soon they wanted to hear from their potential architect.

All I could think of was how on earth, regardless of how successfully we'd done anything, would these men know that my team could be trusted to lead the design portion of their project? I said the only thing I could think of to say.

"What types of things would the church need from us?"

The group began patiently reporting research, data, information, and projections as to what their needs might be. I listened as they described their vision for an open, welcoming place where young families would feel safe settling in to raise their children and committing to the church's many ministries. Their vision was extremely clear, although I could immediately tell there was much work to be done. They had no drawings or sketches. I asked if we could meet again in a week to go over some thoughts we would have in response.

For the next week, we mobilized as if the job were ours. We put four different people on the job of conceptually solving their puzzle four different ways—that is, working out a program, sketching a site plan, and laying out a simple floor plan based on all of their needs. One week later, we presented the ideas to the church. In a little over an hour, we were hired. The church told us it was the most valuable hour they'd spent in two years.

From our side, the interaction benefitted us because we were able to get to know the group better by engaging in a real conversation about their vision and what would best serve the causes they had at hand. We bring to the table an ability to see what's coming around the corner for a church when it comes to the construction industry. It is very valuable to our team to have the chance to see if a church will acknowledge and heed good advice.

From the church's perspective, the interaction benefitted them in two ways. One, they too were able to get to know our team personally and see if we were a good working fit. Did we communicate in a similar style as they did? Were we able to bring value to the table which they didn't already have, both in terms of skillset and strategy? And last, they were able to make real use of the information we compiled for discussion.

I determined on the way home from that meeting that this was really what all churches needed—a reasonably-priced test drive. Early on in the planning, they needed an opportunity to see what a team was made of and how capable they were of creating a built environment in response to the vision of the church.

And once that test drive proved the partnership would work, the church needed that team to plug in for the long haul. If you had the choice, would you wait until the actual design and construction phases to have that valuable conversation? On the contrary, it would be better to have a strategy session once a year. Often, the traditional methods of design professionals working with churches are always reacting, always responding, and for the first time it seemed possible for churches to operate proactively.

WHAT'S THE NORM ON ARCHITECTS AND CONTRACTORS?

For the record, there are many traditional ways to hire an architect and a contractor. You can hire the architect, work for a year, shelve the drawings, then come back, interview contractors, and break ground. You can hire a "design-build" firm, where the architect often works for the contractor. You can hire an architect and then hire a construction manager during design who will review the drawings for buildability. All are notable methods that can work well.

But as it pertains to the church, there are major flaws in these systems. When a contractor works under an architect, the problems typically revolve around budget. The architect listens to the church, makes a list of everything they need, and then draws the building plans. The challenge here is that the architect doesn't have the contractor's input at this critical stage of development. Some architects can also tend to get carried away with beautiful touches here and there that drive up the cost. However, when an architect works for a contractor, problems also arise. The architect is the individual bound by a license to the state to protect the health, safety, and welfare of the public. Regardless of what a church's budget may or may not be, buildings have to follow codes without exception. This is not to say contractors do not care about codes, but they are not legally responsible, and therefore, their focus is usually elsewhere. The general problem with either scenario is that the two "arms" should have equal responsibility and authority—in fact, in ancient times, those roles were actually fulfilled by one person. Now the roles are operating separately in a world where prices are high, labor is short, codes are out of control, and churches are growing and need to move in yesterday.

It is very important in discussions such as these to set personal feelings and preferences aside for the sake of best practices and objectivity. Remember that as we discuss our own experiences here, we are speaking only to these matters as they pertain to *churches*. These thoughts are virtually irrelevant to the construction of a public project such as a school or maybe a hospital, for example. So as the industry pertains to churches, a major detriment to the project occurs when the lack of a properly integrated process between the two professions (architecture and construction) yields waste—wastes of time, of money, and of resources. In my experience, traditional design and construction methods create waste for churches as well as the teams working for them. This happens repeatedly as an architect works on a project all the way through design, only to discover that means, methods, or price will not work. This waste occurs as a contractor prices a job repeatedly, making cuts to get to a budget which was never within reach in the very beginning. And the waste occurs for the church, as the committee drains its energy and funds in vain toward goals which were ill-advised.

In the case of construction, costs go up every day—the info you heard two years ago is most likely no longer valid. The key word to focus on here is "plan." If you can get your mind focused on your overall vision, and if you can form solid, sober expectations, you can expect success.

So, how is this accomplished?

A STRATEGY THAT GETS ANSWERS

In order to make decisions based on solid advice, you need to begin a search, preferably early on, for **partners.*** If possible, find your church's partners—an architect and a contractor—at the same time, and make sure they are also invested in being partners with each other. When you hire an architect first (or a contractor who then hires an architect in a design-build relationship), the second person to be hired usually has to play catch-up on the project details, and you lose critical input from them. And when one works for the other (or even answers to one another, such as in the most traditional Owner-Architect-Contractor relationship), none of the parties can truly act as partners, due to the very nature of the relationship.

> If you can get your mind focused on your overall vision, and if you can form solid, sober expectations, you can expect success.

Why is it so vital that you, your architect, and your contractor act as partners? Consider the very definition and meaning of "partner"; a

---

* **partner**—one who shares the common goal, divides risk, and works diligently toward the success of the group.

CHURCH's Responsibilites:
- Vision
- Budget
- Property conditions
- Prompt payment
- Prompt response to
  questions/issues
  during all phases
- Actions of church/
  committee

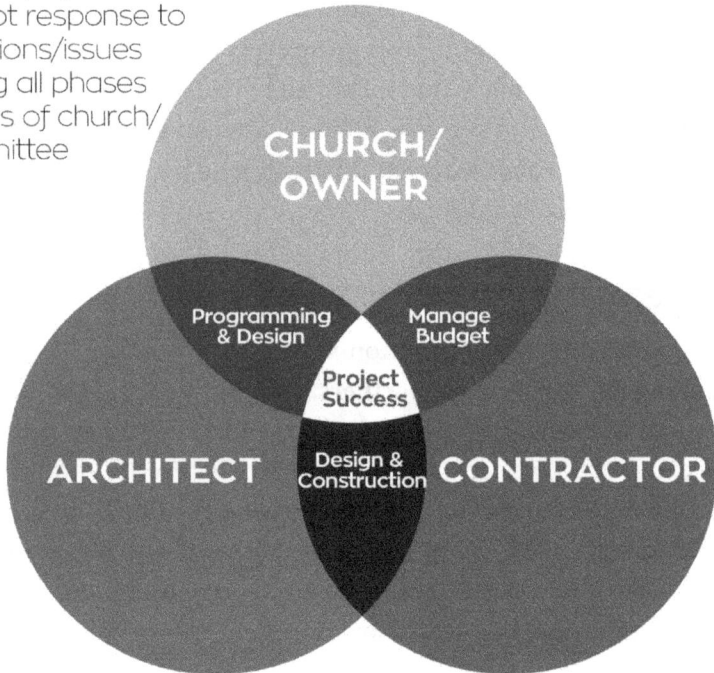

CHURCH/ OWNER

Programming & Design

Manage Budget

Project Success

ARCHITECT

Design & Construction

CONTRACTOR

ARCHITECT's Responsibilities:
- Create Design
- Produce drawings
- Code compliance
- Civil Engineer
- Structural Engineer
- Mechanical/Electrical/
  Plumbing Engineers
- Provide drawing clarifications
- Construction administration
- Schedule

CONTRACTOR's Responsibilities:
- Budget/Estimating
- Constructability reviews
- Site Investigations
- Construction
- Means
- Methods
- Insurance
- Safety
- Subcontractor coordination
- Schedule

RESPONSIBILITY DIAGRAM
CHURCH **ARCHITECT CONTRACTOR**

partner is *one who shares*. A partner is one of a group of people who play together in a game against an opposing side. A partner avoids using the words "us" and "them," which can create division on a team. A partner brings every resource they have to the table. A partner expects a benefit from the relationship, and they are fully invested in the total success of the group. Partners have an interest in making sure all partners stay in the loop, so they are willing to take extra efforts to communicate openly and clearly. A partner can get over another partner's mistakes at times, because of the immense value that his partner brings to the group.

We are in no way suggesting that you form a legal partnership between yourself (the church) and any design or construction companies. In fact, we are typically against legal partnerships even between architects and contractors themselves because such arrangements are very rarely able to keep a decent set of checks and balances in play. What I am suggesting is that you build a team of partners for the church who are invested in longevity, full disclosure, and trust. I am suggesting you participate actively in the success of your partners as they participate in yours. Form the type of relationship with these professionals where you could even ask if their services are needed and trust you would get an honest answer, because they believe in the value of the relationship first.

WHAT IS THE VALUE TO THE CHURCH?

So who are these people, and what do they do? When should they be involved, and at what points should they be responsible for something?

Let's start with who is actually responsible for what.

We want to suggest this general rule of thumb for dividing responsibilities: *if you bring the value to the table, you are responsible*.

Let's begin with the church. You are responsible for communicating your vision to the partners. You are responsible for the actions and behavior of your committee and congregation as it pertains to the project. You are responsible for prompt payment to your partners on a regular basis. You are responsible for the property you own and any unforeseen characteristics of that property.

Now let's talk first about the architect's team. On this team you will have an **Architect of Record** (typically the owner or a principal in their company). This is the individual who holds the license for the seal on your construction drawings. On the architect's team, this is the person responsible by law for the health, safety, and welfare of the public who enter your building. You may also have a Project Architect or Designer who will work directly on your drawings, a Project Manager who will be in close communication with you throughout the project, and a Draftsman (who could also be an intern working toward licensure). These people will communicate and talk about your project even more than you do.

Also on your architect's team, although likely not part of their actual company, will be a team of **professional engineers**. Your architect should have final say in who these individuals are, and you can either pay the engineers as part of your contract with the architect or the architect can help you create an agreement to compensate them individually. On most projects for new construction or renovation, you will have a **civil engineer** (handling everything to do with designing the site, detaining water, paving, etc.), a **structural engineer** (charged with designing the foundation and structure of the building), and an **MEP Engineer** (this usually stands for a group of three engineers and includes the **Mechanical Engineer, Electrical Engineer**, and **Plumbing Engineer**).

These are the people most actively involved during the design phase of your project. Check out the diagram to see how this relates to a typical church's project schedule.

Let's walk through why you need an architect partner:

1. To **program** your needs and arrive at the optimal amount of square footage the church needs to operate with room for growth
2. To design the building (including the site, the plan, and the way it looks on the outside and the inside) and to consider the impact of your building at every level: the person, the church, and the community
3. To get your **engineers** together, to inform them about the building goals and the budget, and to make sure all of their drawings work with the intent of the project

OWNER TEAM MOBILIZATION

O: Locate Project Partners

O: Assemble Committee

O: Complete Needs Research

O: Investigate Budget Paramaters

2-3 mo.

EARLY PHASE PLANNING

O: Communicate Vision

A: Advise as Needed

C: Advise as Needed

2-3 mo.

LAND/ PROPERTY SEARCH

O: Work with Realtor to Search for Property

A: Feasibility Studies

C: Budget/Feasibility Reviews

1-12 mo.

NEGOTIATION/ VETTING

O: Negotiations

A: Site Investigations

C: Site Investigations

1-3 mo.

DESIGN DEVELOPMENT

O: Communicate Specific Use Needs

A: Refine Project Requirements

C: Cost Estimating

2 mo.

SCHEMATIC DESIGN

O: Communicate Vision

A: Define Scope & Concept

C: Preliminary Budgets Concept

3 mo.

MASTER PLANNING

O: Determine Goals/Dreams

A: Create Master Plan

C: Constructability Strategy

2 mo.

PROGRAMMING

O: Define Wants & Needs

A: Produce Program

C: Advise as Needed

1-3 mo.

CONSTRUCTION DOCUMENTS

O: Review Check Sets

A: Produce Construction Documents

C: Consult on Systems, Constructibility

2 mo.

ACCESSIBILITY REVIEW

O: Assist Team on Forms

A: Submit Project to TDLR

C: Consult

1/2 mo.

PERMITTING

O: Assist Team on Forms/Permitting Conditions

A: Acquire Necessary Permits

C: Acquire Necessary Permits

1-3 mo.

BIDDING

O: Review Bids

A: Addenda/ Questions

C: Put Project out for Bid

1 1/2 mo.

OWNER OCCUPANCY

O: Occupy Building!

A: Final Walk

C: Record Drawings, Certificate of Occupancy

1/2 mo.

OWNER MOVE - IN

O: Move in!

A: Inspections

C: Punch Work

1/2 mo.

CONSTRUCTION

O: Decisions

A: Construction Administration

C: Manage Construction

9-18 mo.

CONSTRUCTION MOBILIZATION

O: Communication

A: Create Posted Set

C: Mobilize/Set Schedule

1/2 mo.

O: CHURCH/OWNER RESPONSIBILITIES

A: ARCHITECT RESPONSIBILITIES

C: CONTRACTOR RESPONSIBILITIES

SAMPLE PROJECT PHASE SCHEDULE
CHURCH ARCHITECT CONTRACTOR
Responsibilities/Contributions

4. To make sure your building meets codes regarding health, safety, and welfare of the public because you are renovating/building a commercial building. To communicate with your city's local authorities on your behalf.

5. During construction, to act on the church's behalf in relaying the church's intent for the building (that is, how the church wants to use it and what you want it to be like), as related to interpreting the drawing set.

6. To advise on matters of process during the design and construction phases.

In the best of cases, you should have a relationship of complete honesty and openness with the architect's team. You should be able to tell them when they are missing the mark without hurting their feelings, and you should be able to accept when they suggest that you push back your schedules, or that your budget expectations are off. Sometimes architects even help you consider ways your ministries could work more efficiently. Your architect will probably be the only person besides you who will obsess over every detail of how the dream is going to play out. So tell them your whole story. Be intentional about verbalizing your biggest dream for the church and certainly tell the whole truth about your budget possibilities. The more accurate information your architect has, the better they can help you during these critical early planning stages.

If you have not been through a construction project in the past, you need to be prepared for the leadership roles to change throughout the process. From the planning stage through design and permitting, you will need to rely on the architect's team as the authority on codes, design expertise, and engineering coordination. During this time, the construction partner needs to serve in a support role, offering cost info and building system knowledge and serving as an extra pair of experienced eyes on the developing drawing set. Once the project moves from bidding into construction, the architect will immediately shift into a support role as the contractor takes responsibility for managing the project forward.

If you have not been through a construction project in the past, you need to be prepared for the leadership roles to change throughout the process.

So what value does your **construction team** offer the church?

1. Cost. They'll tell you the price of items, which will help you set a reasonable budget upfront. If you are late to the game in establishing a realistic budget, they'll get you back on track to accomplish what is feasible for the church by providing **phased solutions** or **strategic plans.**

2. A seasoned construction manager can drive enough competition to your bid to generate at least 10–15% of savings from what you could achieve on your own.

3. **Methods.** Contractors know the *methods* we need to use to build. Architects can draw the building you want, but someone actually has to get out in the dirt and put this giant beast together. Contractors know how.

4. **Means.** They have the means to get the work done. They have the list of tradespeople, and they have the equipment. They know who to call and when. They've got men willing to wake up at 3:00 a.m. and supervise concrete pours, work all day, and then come back and do the same thing tomorrow.

5. Insurance and safety programs. They use their people trained in building and supervising to keep your job site safe and the church free of liability while tons of steel hang overhead and electricians do their work, among other dangerous tasks.

For all practical purposes, the church needs to stay in a decision-making role throughout, acting as property owner and authority over the church's funds and overall vision implementation.

During Design:

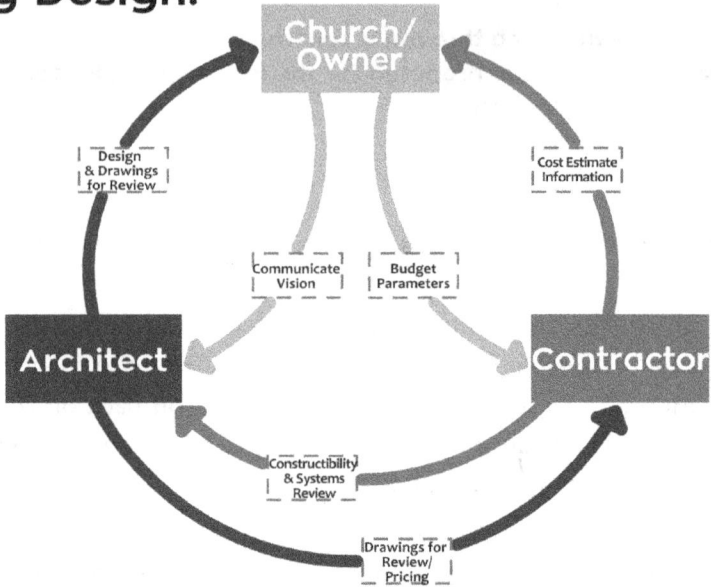

Church/Owner

Design & Drawings for Review

Cost Estimate Information

Communicate Vision

Budget Parameters

Architect

Contractor

Constructibility & Systems Review

Drawings for Review/Pricing

During Construction:

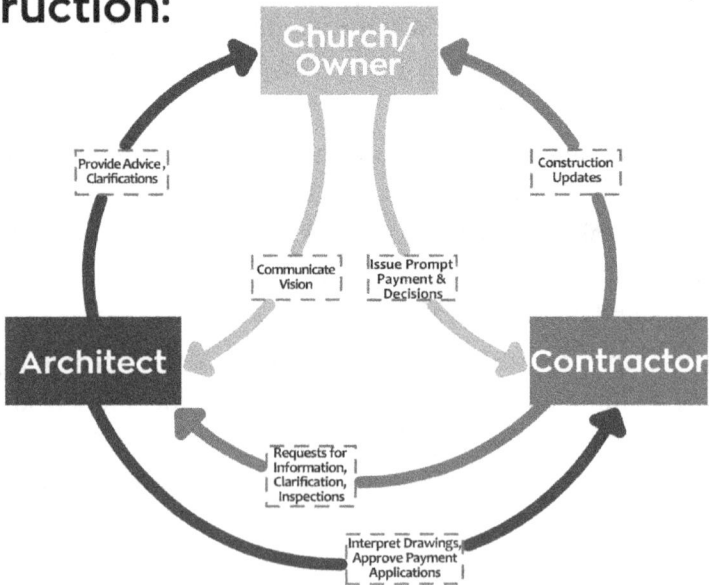

Church/Owner

Provide Advice, Clarifications

Construction Updates

Communicate Vision

Issue Prompt Payment & Decisions

Architect

Contractor

Requests for Information, Clarification, Inspections

Interpret Drawings, Approve Payment Applications

COMMUNICATION CHECKS & BALANCES
CHURCH **ARCHITECT** CONTRACTOR

Note: *If your contractor or architect is not pulling their weight or has demonstrated an inability or unwillingness to take care of business, you will need to take action. Do not adopt a "turn the other cheek" mindset. If you are faced with a situation where there is negligence, take immediate action to meet with the elders and begin conversations to get back on track or to end the relationship. By using the methods outlined here, though, this scenario is highly unlikely.*

HOW MUCH DO THESE PARTNERS COST, MIGHT I ASK?

So it's evident, both by law (as all church construction projects are required to have a licensed architect onboard), and now by the responsibilities detailed in this book, that every church needs a professional team of both architect and contractor as partners. The main question now is, how much do these services cost and when do you actually need to have the funds ready to go?

ARCHITECT'S FEES

As a starting place for discussion, architectural services unrelated to a specific building project (such as planning, city research, master planning, feasibility studies, AutoCAD drawing, rendering, etc.) are typically charged as either a lump sum price for the specific service, or hourly according to a schedule which your architect can provide you.

Expect that the Architect of Record or a principal in an office will be one of the highest paid individuals, with a senior licensed architect having a similar hourly rate. A draftsman or assistant capable of providing you with the same services you need will obviously come at a lower rate. If you are asking for these types of services, a simple proposal letter stating your agreement is suitable. The architect's office should provide this to the church for signature. Do not expect your partner to commence work before you have signed an agreement, even if you have a strong past working relationship. In many cases, a retainer fee, even in the case of hourly or a lump sum arrangement, is standard practice and expectation. It is most common that you would be billed monthly for these fees, and that your invoice would show a running total of your arrangement explaining what you've paid and what you owe.

In the case of a construction project, be that a renovation or a new construction project, most architects will charge you a percentage of the cost of construction. Generally speaking, this percentage includes at least some of the professional engineers you also need for the project. Historically, the "A/E fee," or "architect's/engineer's" fee, was a percentage which included the architect, the structural engineer, the mechanical engineer, the electrical engineer, the plumbing engineer, and sometimes the civil engineer. Today, this varies greatly based on the project, owner, and architectural firm. You'll need to ask specifically about each of these trades when discussing the compensation plan for your architect's team. You can expect a fee of 7–10% for an experienced church architect's team, with sole practitioners being at the low end of the percentages and very large teams being at the upper end of the range or beyond.

Your architect's fee is going to depend largely on the type of project you have at hand. A renovation takes more time, period. You need to expect to pay more for an architect to painstakingly decipher how to handle a renovation of an older building, especially a repurpose type of project. These types of projects also typically require significantly more engineering than new construction.

So, when are these fees due? Let's walk through a very simple scenario, but first we need to have a common understanding of these general principles in the industry:

1. You will receive a monthly bill.
2. You are going to be billed based on how much work has been completed to date.
3. It is very common that a retainer is part of the compensation plan, and you will owe that upon signing the agreement in order for the team to get started.
4. "Additional services" are fees that do not relate to the actual design of the building (for example, copies and plans for presentations, trips to the printer where the architect creates and prints boards

for fundraising, etc.). Your contract will address how you will deal with these as they come up.

5. You are purchasing services, not drawings. The drawings will be created for the construction of your project (and you are paying for this use). With very few exceptions, the architectural drawings themselves are the intellectual property of the architectural firm.

6. There are several "phases" of the design phase, and these are common to the industry-standard AIA contract (contracts created and approved by the American Institute of Architects). The general phases are: **schematic design** (SD), **design development** (DD), **construction documents** (CD), **bidding** (B) and **construction administration** (CA).

7. For each of these phases, the AIA Contract assigns a percentage to that phase indicating about *how much of the total design project takes place in that phase.* For example, the "Schematic Design" Phase is considered to be 25% *of the work of the total design project.*

(**Note:** *All of the design phases are defined for quick reference in the glossary, but schematic design typically means you have all agreed on what the basic site plan, floor plan, and elevation is going to look like!*)

Now, let's say for clear illustration that your building renovation cost is $1,000,000. You have entered into a contractual agreement with your architect where the A/E team's fee is 7%. In your case, this fee includes all of the engineers you need for the project. You have also agreed to a 10% retainer so that the architect can enter into agreements with all of the engineers on your behalf. Your project *design schedule* is for a duration of 6 months. Here's an example of how this process may work:

- You understand that ultimately, your financial commitment to the architect is $70,000 in fees, not including any additional services ($1 million project x 7%).

- You meet up with the architect to pass off the signed contract (be sure to get a scanned copy!), and drop off their retainer check to get them started. The retainer check, for 10% of the architect's fee, should be $7,000. Let's assume your retainer is refundable.

- Of the $70,000, you have paid the architect $7,000 and still owe $63,000, which will be billed to you throughout the next six months and then throughout construction.
- At the end of the first month, you receive a bill for 25% of the Schematic Design Phase. Should you agree that you are about a quarter of the way through SD, this is what you need to figure:
  - Remember (from above) that the Schematic Design phase is 25% of the total *design project*, or 25% x $70,000= $17,500.
  - So the cost for the SD phase is $17,500, and you are a quarter of the way through SD.
  - You should be billed 25% x $17,500, or $4,375 for the first month.
- Your bill should show you that you have previously paid $7,000, and that you owe $4,375.

Now, let's say during the month you needed a fundraising board and you asked the architect to design this for you, have it professionally printed, pick it up from the printer, and drop it off at the church. You would expect to see these costs on your bill as well. Definitely let your architect know you'd like to discuss these types of fees prior to incurring them, even though they are technically in your contract.

CONSTRUCTION MANAGER'S FEES

The most common question we hear pertaining to church design and construction is, "Do we need to have all of the funding for the project ready to go when we start design?" The answer is no. To begin *design*, you need the amount of the design cost (typically a percentage of the construction cost). To begin *construction,* you need access to the funds for the building cost.

Thankfully, the construction manager's fee structure is typically much more straightforward than the fee structure of the design phase. However, during construction you will owe significantly larger sums of money than in the design phase (the building is finally going up!).

It is prior to construction when most churches confirm all lending agreements, pledges, and other contributions to ensure that the invoices will be paid on time.

Before construction begins (that is, before you have a contract for construction with your construction manager and a building permit), you should enter into a letter-type agreement with your construction partner to outline how you will compensate them fairly for their responsibilities and services during planning and design. Services such as site investigation, building investigation, asbestos inspections, city coordination, budget and estimating services, scheduling strategies, and means and methods consulting are key parts of the design process, but they are typically simple, lower-cost services. A letter agreement will clarify compensation.

When you and your construction manager agree to a cost of the project, they will most typically expect to be paid a percentage of the construction cost, comparable to the same range of the architect's fee. In most cases, the construction manager's fee is included in the *building cost*, and certainly in the project cost. Some construction managers require a retainer and others do not (many times, depending on the type of project and the familiarity with the customer).

After you agree to a cost for the building and any additional project costs, you will sign a contract with the construction manager. This contract is strictly between you and the construction partner, but the architect's contract is tied to this contract in the following ways:

- The architect is required by law to participate in construction administration, or remove his/her seal from a commercial project.
- The architect will approve the construction manager's Application for Payment (this is their monthly invoice to the church as mentioned in Chapter 5), as well as approve other milestones such as **Substantial Completion.***

---

* **substantial completion**—the stage of construction when the work is sufficiently complete and ready for the church to move into the building [according to a standard AIA (American Institute of Architects) contract].

What you can expect on this invoice is a running tab of work that's been completed onsite, materials which are onsite or stored offsite, as well as work done by individual trades. The construction manager's fee will be added to these monthly invoices as line items, and you will owe the total each month.

Absolutely critical to the project is a reliable process where the church reviews the pay app promptly and creates a systematic method to pay on time every month (provided you agree that the work has been done). If for whatever reason you do not think you agree, certainly bring this up to the construction manager immediately and ask for an explanation. Questions for clarification of any type are always appreciated, and usually a conversation is all that is needed. If you are convinced after a conversation with the construction manager that a pay app is in error, you should discuss the issue as a group with the architect, who is most typically charged with approving the pay apps. If the church is in disagreement with both parties, hold a meeting with the building committee and/or the elders as quickly as possible so as not to slow the project. Regardless of who is right or wrong, all partners should have a vested interest in completing the project and certainly making sure that all trades who have completed work are paid fairly and on time.

OKAY, HOW DO I FIND THESE PEOPLE?

If you live in an urban area, a quick Google search will yield a high number of "possibilities" for architects and contractors. If your church is in a rural area, there's a good chance you are familiar with the architects and contractors in your town. What you are looking for, primarily, are partners with experience specifically in church campus design and construction. This aspect is critically important. What is *not* critically important is whether or not that church is the same denomination as you are, or whether they have the same type of music situation as you do. Far more critical is a company's mindset and experience dealing with the specific needs of churches in general.

Whether a firm will provide advice and reasonably-priced "test drive" services for a church speaks volumes about their culture and mindset.

There is very little (if any at all) financial payoff to a professional who pours information into a church for an hourly rate of compensation. An architect or contractor who will provide these services for a reasonable cost upfront is likely more interested in a long-term partnership than the immediate gain of projects that will fuel company cash flow. For this reason alone, firms who offer small introductory services are almost always a better fit for a church project because they are willing to acknowledge and respond to the specific needs of a church.

The other sign of a firm who is naturally more responsive to a church's needs is one who openly acknowledges its need for a partner along the way. An architect who understands the value of a construction partner *from day one*, and vice versa, is a sign of a firm interested in a more inclusive, value-oriented, project-centered environment. When discussing your project with architects, ask them what their usual methods are in working with construction managers. If they truly believe in working closely with construction managers, they will bring this subject up in initial conversations.

Some architects and contractors will offer this type of partnership arrangement upon request, while others (such as my own company) believe strongly enough in the concept to limit their work to *only* partnership arrangements. Can a company have multiple strategic partnerships? For instance, could a contractor work with a certain architect on some projects and another on others? *Absolutely.* This concept is in no way about exclusivity. The concept is about avoiding waste, adding value to a project, and being intentional when choosing partners, reducing risk for everyone.

> An architect who understands the value of a construction partner *from day one*, and vice versa, is a sign of a firm interested in a more inclusive, value-oriented, project-centered environment.

As you search for the right architect, start in your immediate community of churches. Look for people you know (or know through others) who have completed recent successful projects. Do a little networking and ask around your general geographical area. Generally speaking, 100 to 150 miles is a good maximum radius to expect great results from your partners. They do not need to be in your backyard, but travel to a meeting should not be prohibitive either. The more sophisticated a company's makeup is, the farther they will be able to mobilize for a project. Look for architects or contractors in your general area with a good reputation for designing or building churches, and look for churches *who are pleased and happy with the process and the overall results.*

Who does your church leadership know in the construction industry? Do you know any firms who specialize in church design or construction or who have demonstrated excellent performance in this field?

If you do know someone (or if you've heard of someone who has successfully completed church projects in your area), research their company before reaching out to them. Look at their projects on their website and on social media.

As a rule of thumb, you'll want to confirm that the firms you are interested in have projects in various stages: completed, in design, and in construction. This indicates a healthy company who can sustain their teams with an appropriate amount of work and resources to fuel growth and new technologies in the field. When you find a company or companies you feel might be a good fit, call the churches listed on their website.

Here is a trick: Do not call a firm and ask for references. Companies will give you only the names of the best people they have worked with— they will not give you the names of clients who would tell you something negative! Instead, look on their website and call the people they've worked for. Do not call one church; in order to gain a well-rounded understanding, you must contact as many references as possible.

Introduce yourself and ask to speak to the pastor. Tell him you are at the very beginning stages of your search for a church architect (or contractor) and ask if you could discuss their project with the person who served as the church's representative during design and construction. In almost all cases they will be more than happy to refer you. Call this person directly and ask if there is a good time to talk so that they do not feel rushed and can communicate as much as possible. If you are researching a contractor, also ask the church for the name of the architect who worked on the project, and vice versa. You'll learn more with this method than with any proposal or interview.

Visit www.churchbuildingguide.com for a list of referral questions.

Try to get a good feel for the type of person you are speaking to on the phone before you begin asking them your questions. Some good conversation starters are to ask them how long they've been at the church, what they do for a living, etc., before launching into a building project. You'll get a feel for their demeanor. An extremely quiet, reserved person might describe a great contractor as "fine," whereas a very excitable person could easily over-convey a company's credentials. Just be aware that you really do need to speak with several people. The likely outcome of these conversations is that you will hear both positives and negatives, and many times even positives and negatives about one company. Usually, names of certain companies (whether the ones you initially called about or others) will surface as very good options. You'll want to visit with your committee and compare notes, and then make a decision about which company or companies to contact.

In this way, you are choosing your team based entirely on a referral system: the churches referred you to them, and they are also referring you to the other design/construction partner.

SETTING UP THE MEETING

Call the company you are interested in and ask for a meeting. Explain that you have researched their firm and have spoken with the owners of some of their projects. You'd like to tell them what you have going on and see if they are interested in the work, whether that be small, up-front services or full project. Ask if they'd be willing to bring their best option for an architect/contractor with them to the meeting. (If you got the names of both an architect and contractor who have worked together, invite them both to the same meeting.)

During this meeting, your main objective is to determine if the parties are good candidates to begin a relationship with the church. Block about an hour and a half for such a meeting and appoint a member of your team to keep time. Allow yourself 20 or so minutes to explain the church's position, and then ask the architect/contractor how they would handle a project such as yours. (Consider bringing some of the tools you've worked through, such as your vision plan and other relevant documents.)

Once you've presented your story, let the architect and contractor respond sufficiently. Here is what you're listening for from the architect and contractor:

- Evidence of their experience working together, preferably on church projects (e.g., "We've done multiple projects together.")
- An easy back-and-forth conversation of information between the two companies (very little "us" and "them").
- If you gave them at least several days' notice, it's a good sign if they prepared something for you to take away, such as a packet of references or list of projects.
- A general demeanor of helpfulness and interest in what *you* have going on, rather than telling you everything you could ever need to know about their own setup.
- A willingness to provide up-front services and advice, at a reasonable cost, with the understanding that you are interested in creating a partnership to take you through the project and further.
- A discussion indicating how they can work cost concerns in your favor (bidding processes, etc.).
- A comfort level with differing opinions. (Prepare yourself, architects and contractors often have to work through constructive conflict to arrive at the correct answer!) Watch for a demeanor of respect for opinions differing from their own.
- An engagement in your project conversation as it relates to other work they have done. There is no substitute for experience.

While meeting, you will of course want to ask about price. Generally, you should expect there to be a reasonable range of compensation for architects and contractors who provide these types of services (7–10% of the building cost for the architect's team depending on which engineers are included, and about the same percentage for the contractor). These fees, when applied to a construction budget, can be large sums of money. However, when factoring in the amount of money saved by a contractor who knows how to navigate bidding, and dollars saved in design by an architect who chooses engineers wisely and brings industry experience in the use of economical materials, the actual professional fees paid to your partners are a very sound investment. For projects not yet in design or construction phases, fees should be either lump sum prices for services, or simple hourly rates to get small tasks done for you.

One important note to keep in mind: do not focus your energies on debating small differences in the price and making elaborate comparisons between companies. Once you've established that the potential candidates are within the acceptable range, focus on what they tell you about their process and experience. You could save tens of thousands (and even hundreds of thousands on larger jobs) by using a company with resources and excellent strategies. Their expertise should be the deciding factor, not minor variances in price.

Note that there is a difference between this strategy and the act of conducting a formal interview process. An **interview**, in the context of building projects, is a somewhat formal event used for the purpose of selecting the most qualified applicant for a project. While an excellent tool in many arenas, a typical interview process works counterproductively for a church project. Here's why.

Candidates for the job put great preparations into an interview, spending hours compiling information to make them look good in the hopes of being hired for a project. The very nature of a formal interview lends itself to more of a "first date" experience rather than a real understanding of a team's strengths and weaknesses. (In publicly funded building projects, interviews are sometimes the only legal option. But, you are privately funded. You can do what you want and hire who you want, for better or for worse.)

Instead, it is more beneficial for a church to sit down and have a *real conversation about your vision and your projects* and gauge the capabilities, interest, and response of the architect and contractor. Will we, PlanNorth, participate in an interview in hopes of being hired for a project? Of course. If we're interested in the project, *and if we're able to bring a construction partner to the table,* we will come to an interview. We will bring some materials about our company and do our best to answer whatever questions the church has. But the truth is, we just want to hear about the project and meet the church personally, so that we can quickly determine whether our team is a good fit. If not, we will introduce them to someone who might be a better fit. A good architect, and certainly a good contractor, is probably not overly skilled at putting on a dog and pony show. They want to hear about your project and see if their company should collaborate with you.

Handle the situation as general business and call a meeting to discuss the possibility of the mutually beneficial relationships at hand. These people are your potential partners, so you should act intentionally. If you realize after meeting that it will not work out, no harm, no foul. Call them immediately to thank them for their time and to relay the message. Follow up with a thank you in the mail and keep their contact info. You never know when a respectful meeting which did not work for one situation may be a perfect fit for another. Be sure to pass on the contact info for reputable companies to other churches; a referral is the greatest sign of appreciation to any business.

Visit www.churchbuildingguide.com to download a sample "first meeting" agenda.

The goal of your meeting is to begin a partnership between two teams and the church under either an agreement for simple services or for design/construction for a building project. It may take several meetings with several companies to find the best fit. The long-term goal is to work toward a partnership which will carry the church (and the two companies) into a permanent working relationship where the partners can call on each other for advice, referrals, and quick information that will benefit the church. Clearly, such relationships take time and energy to cultivate. Such is the nature of church facilities, though, and that is the reason this approach is the best solution for all.

If you are ready to hire an architect and contractor to design and construct your facility, note that you will also want to ask the teams to submit a more thorough amount of information to prove their capabilities. Items you need to request from both the architect and contractor are as follows:

- Copies of insurance (both companies)
- A completed jobs list, with jobs completed together specifically marked
- A "jobs in progress" list, showing square footage and dollar amounts
- A documented **safety plan*** (from the contractor only)
- Proof of **bonding capacity*** (from contractor only)
- A list of references willing to discuss the team's work
- The architect's general design philosophy (this will tell you more than you think!). Look for signs that an architect has a heart *and an understanding* of ministry work.
- Sample contracts for both parties (these contracts should be separate agreements, one between the church and the architect and another between the church and the contractor)

Ideally, your new construction and architect "partners" have worked together many times. These professionals are evaluating the church's leadership team as well. They should be evaluating your ability to make decisions reasonably and maintain clear lines of communication and chain of command. As harsh as it may sound, professional relationships that don't pass muster during the test-drive period are a blessing to both sides. A talented professional will focus his best efforts on customers who are focused on their vision and have their act together. A church that is serious about growth will tolerate only excellent services from their partners.

---

* **safety plan**—a contractor's plan for keeping your jobsite safe. This plan should include their safety rules and training procedures.

* **bonding capacity**—the maximum amount a bonding company will extend to a contractor in performance bonds, minus the sum of all contract amounts which the company currently has bonded. (Should a contractor fail to complete a project, a project which has a bond will be completed by the bond company or another contractor hired by the bond company.)

When you find the right partners, the advantage to all involved is virtually priceless. You have someone you can call on for solid advice. You now have experts on your team and a team you can charge with vetting ideas, properties, expansion possibilities, and even new construction. Because you are an educated customer respectful of their time and talents, you are now an extremely valuable asset to your partners. Over time, they will become professionally invested in the success of your church; that is, you will get their very best advice. When there is a new resource or product, you will know first. Your church will get their best consultants, their best creative talent, their deepest discounts, and their best teams. Why? That's easy. You will get their best because their other customers *hired* them, and you *partnered* with them. You will continue to trust them and bring them business over time, so *you* are the most valued customer. Putting in the time to research and create a strong partnership will richly benefit everyone involved.

As I wrap up these stories and thoughts, I am reminded of a note I have on the wall above my desk. It has hung in the same location since our firm moved to a studio downtown a couple of years ago, and I seem to consider it for a moment every morning:

> *The mind that opens to a new idea never returns to its original size.*
>
> –Albert Einstein

Those words continue to inspire me every day, reminding me to constantly search for better solutions and processes.

Our churches have taught us priceless lessons about architecture, about ministry, and about people. These lessons are the reason we love designing churches: for every piece of advice or line drawn, our team is blessed ten-fold by the company of the customers we keep. I want to share a story with you as we wrap up these conversations:

> *About four years ago we were introduced to a new church plant in our town. The project was very small. The pastor wanted to do an interior remodel to accommodate the children and a fellowship space in an old neighborhood church building they had just*

purchased. Ironically, this building was the same place where I'd been baptized when I was 12 years old. The project was a little surreal, considering that suddenly I could remember every detail of going to church there for many years as a child. We finished up the project, completed our standard first-Sunday attendance to make sure everything was running smoothly after it opened, and went back to business as usual.

But the Lord works in mysterious ways, and within about a year our family felt drawn back to this little church, which by this time wasn't really that little anymore. We eventually became members, and only a couple of months later my husband was baptized in this same church where I was baptized as a child. I don't think about the odds of this very often, because when I do it's too farfetched for me to comprehend.

Fast forward a bit, and our church purchased a "new" building across town in a great location. The pastors found a great deal and jumped on it, but this building is not pretty. For several months, we worked on trying to repurpose this short, wood-framed building to open up an area suitable for a welcoming sanctuary, and we finally got all the "design" pieces in a row for it to work. In the next step, our construction partner would review the plans for cost and buildability. We emailed the ideas over, and I got a call almost immediately. The construction manager advised against our plan because of all the additional expenses associated with opening up a sanctuary in a wood-framed building and updating the HVAC equipment.

We met a week later at a coffee shop to tell our pastor we thought we needed to switch gears. It would be more economical to leave the little building as is (reserving it for classroom spaces, ministry meeting spaces, and offices) and add a new pre-engineered structure to accommodate the sanctuary. Could the church afford to renovate the entire existing building and still build the new one all at once? No way. However, we knew our team would put our heads together and figure it out. We would work toward a phased plan that would allow for later expansion.

Had we not had the advice of the construction partner at that critical step, we would have made the wrong decision. We would have taken the design we had finally "worked out," and there's a 90% chance we would have built it. The church would have come up with the money for the portions they could have afforded, and we would have phased the rest. Had the construction partner been brought on "for construction," he would have been charged with renovating that little building, and none of us would have known that based on cost and buildability, a better solution was just waiting for us to choose it.

We want the very best solutions for our churches. We want honest advice from our partners, whether it's disappointing at certain stages or whether it's exciting. We want our work, whether in ministry, design, or construction, to be fueled by dependable facts we can rely on.

I do not know what will happen with the "ugly" building. But I know we have the right team in place to give the church leadership the best information at the right time. At this early stage in planning, the only thing that's definite is the vision of the church—that is, the integral mission and culture of the people and their ministries. And that knowledge, *the vision of the church*, is the most far-reaching factor of all.

I will leave you with these big-picture takeaways:

1. Know your vision
2. Understand your responsibilities
3. Educate yourself
4. Find your partners

I hope that the spaces where your church will live and grow are a joy to create.

Action Items:

1. Get out a map and draw a 100–150 mile radius around your church's location. Your search for professional partners should most likely happen within that geographical area.

2. Make a list of churches you know have been successful in their planning and vision casting efforts. Create a plan to contact these churches and search for potential partners who will walk alongside your church for the long haul, assisting with planning and strategy.

3. Download and edit the Sample List of Partner Referral Questions at www.churchbuildingguide.com. Have a team discussion about which questions will lead to the information most important to your church's project/planning.

4. Download the Sample First Meeting Agenda for your church's meeting with industry professionals (www.churchbuildingguide.com).

Discussion Topics:

1. What are the possibilities for funding construction or renovation projects at your church? _____

_____

_____

_____

2. Which is more in alignment with your church culture: a traditional interview or a meeting to get to know potential partners? From your perspective, what are the potential positives and negatives? _____

_____

_____

_____

_____

3. How could a strategy session with industry professionals help you gather information and sort your options for growth? What are the top questions you might ask, if you had the opportunity?

- _____

- _____

- _____

- _____

4. Is your leadership team comfortable in the role as decision-maker throughout a project? More telling, are you comfortable in your ability to support your partners in doing their jobs, versus assuming their responsibilities? What are some of your reservations in staying in a decision-making role? _____

    _____

    _____

    _____

Recap: In almost all cases, the investment in your church's facilities is the single largest expense a church will manage in its lifetime, and for good reason. These spaces are your largest working ministry tool! It is vital to the health of a church's vision that they have access to the input of partners with experience in church building. The best way to find these partners is to rely on the factual accounts of your fellow churches.

CONCLUSION

Some time ago, my friend Joe told me about a project he had been wrestling with for months. The project should have been simple: it was a neighborhood basketball court with a concrete slab and two hoops. However, major controversy in the community had slowed the little basketball court from being built. Joe felt so sure that the youth of the surrounding communities needed the court that he kept after it, playing politics, attending events, and saying the right things to the right people. And although he raised money, I'm pretty sure he also paid for some of the work himself.

A few months later, he asked me if I had seen the basketball court. It was finished! I congratulated him and told him I had seen it and was sure the youth would put it to good use. At the time, I was happy Joe had accomplished his goal; nonetheless my mind was on other things, and I didn't realize how excited he was. But then he said this:

"You know, the other night it was late, cold, and very windy. While I was lying in bed trying to sleep, I starting hearing the bouncing of a ball on the court. I haven't seen a lot of kids on the court yet, and I was thrilled. There was at least one kid playing basketball late at night instead of being out somewhere getting in trouble!"

I could see the clear joy beaming from my friend's face. His mission had been accomplished: one person was off the streets and enjoying the court. The look on Joe's face told me he would do the same work a hundred times if he could help just one more person—a person whom he didn't know and likely never would. The kid bouncing that ball late at night will probably never know the heart of a seventy-year-old man four houses over.

I will never again hear a basketball bounce without remembering the purpose in my friend's eyes. At times, his friends might have grown tired of the saga of the little court, but he pressed on because he knew the court would help the youth in his community. He kept his eyes on the goal.

Some might question the money spent on a basketball court when other people in the community are without basic necessities. How many thousands of lunches could have been prepared with that money? But for my friend Joe, the court wasn't about adding an amenity to sell more people on the community. Instead, the basketball court was about using the built environment as a tool to give the youth something constructive to do, to shape their behavior and decisions, and hopefully to positively affect their life. Joe wanted to invest in strangers' lives and ask nothing in return. He wanted to show love to a neighbor he didn't know.

So many times we hear that church buildings are just a tool. Yes, they are a tool. But "just" a tool? Ask any skilled carpenter how important his tools are, how carefully he selected them, and how much he was willing to invest in those items which would largely determine his capacity for success in his work. The creation of your church's built environment is your single largest opportunity to direct the vision of your ministry.

So, celebrate the journey you are on as you plan your church's facilities, knowing that the work you are doing will touch many lives. When the days are stressful, take a moment to reflect on the reward that these efforts will surely bring to the congregation and to the community. Be encouraged that your efforts will, in fact, bring fruit.

What kind of tools will you create?

GLOSSARY

American Disability Act (ADA)—the law which requires all new construction and renovation projects to make provisions for handicapped persons to use a building in a reasonably equal way to a non-handicapped person.

asbestos—a mineral-type material composed of thin fibers and used widely during the 20th century for construction and buildings. It is now commonly known to cause illness and fatality through exposure, and has been banned for construction purposes.

asbestos inspection—the act of a professionally trained company to inspect an existing building for asbestos. An asbestos inspection will yield either a clean bill for the building in the form of an "asbestos free certificate" or a report indicating how to remove the asbestos safely. There are government-regulated methods and processes for asbestos removal which must be implemented prior to renovations of any kind.

acoustician—an expert in sound engineering who provides specific details of material placement, appropriate wall angles, and other data based on type and number of instruments and voices planned for a worship space.

alternate bids—a bid that calls for an added or subtracted amount from the base number, should alternative materials or methods be selected (Ex: We will bid an upgraded carpet type as an "alternate.").

application for payment (Pay App)—a contractor's typical method of invoice for payment. It provides a method of documenting what items and materials have been provided as well as tracking the current cost of the job.

Architect of Record—the individual whose license/seal appears on a set of construction documents. This person is usually the owner or a principal in an architectural firm.

bidding phase—obtaining individual bids on each portion of the work (painting, electrical, concrete, etc.). It is also referred to as "bidding the job."

bonding capacity—the maximum amount a bonding company will extend to a contractor in performance bonds, minus the sum of all contract amounts which the company currently has bonded. (Should a contractor fail to complete a project, a project which has a bond will be completed by the bond company or another contractor hired by the bond company.)

boundary survey—a survey made only for the purpose of establishing a property's general boundary and requested primarily for land sales and purchases. This survey is typically conducted by locating pins in the ground.

brownfield sites—a piece of industrial or commercial property which is usually being considered for development and has characteristics indicating environmental contamination such as abandoned dump sites, chemical leakage, or abandoned storage of hazardous materials.

building cost—the amount of expenses for the labor, materials, equipment, and contractor's services to build a structure (also referred to as "construction cost" or as "dollars per square foot of building"). These costs do not include the design fees or soft costs.

building envelope requirements—code requirements telling you the amount and type of materials which are allowed as part of your exterior walls and roof systems in order to meet code.

building fund—a designated account (or earmarked funds) for a church's expansion and/or improvements.

building performance—a description of a building's energy efficiency, typically based on the mechanical systems and building envelope properties.

building permit—a document giving a contractor (and his customer, the church) legal permission to build a commercial structure.

capital campaign—multi-year fundraising efforts for a building, reconstruction, remodeling or other major capital improvements. The difference between a capital campaign and general fundraising is the level of focus and effort from dedicated staff and the degree of specific strategy involved in the efforts.

Civil Engineer—a professional engineer who deals with the design and construction of site-related elements such as roads, bridges, parking lots, detention ponds, and paving.

commercial building—as related to church construction, a commercial building is a building which is not residential and is therefore subject to local, state, and federal codes.

construction documents (CDs)—the third and final period of the design phase. During construction documents, the information which has been agreed upon in the previous phases is documented into a set of drawings for construction. It is during CDs that most coordination between the architect's team and the engineers takes place.

construction phase—the phase of the job when the building is built. It begins when a building permit is obtained and when a written contract between a church and a contractor has been signed.

construction team—the portion of the team responsible for building the project, typically composed of a project manager, a project coordinator, estimator(s), and a project superintendent.

contaminants—impure materials/fumes/elements on a site. Many churches will complete due-diligence type testing for contaminants on a site prior to purchase of the land or beginning construction.

contract—a legal agreement between a church and a contractor, a church and an architect, an architect and a consultant, or a contractor and a subcontractor. All of these contracts are necessary pieces of a commercial building project.

design development (DD)—the second period of the design phase. During this phase, the goal is to discover the very specific needs for each space in the building (such as technology, church preferences, acoustics, teaching needs, and kitchen specifics).

design phase—the phase of the project where an architect's team is actively designing a project. The design phase is composed of three distinct periods: schematic design, design development, and construction documents.

detention—as related to building sites, the act of detaining water runoff during a storm for a short period of time and then releasing it back into the watershed, to prevent flooding and excessive runoff. The amount of detention required is directly related to how much impervious development a church builds. **Impervious development** includes surfaces such as concrete where water will run off rather than soaking in naturally. For example, both a concrete sidewalk and a building are impervious surfaces when figuring detention requirements.

DOT (Department of Transportation)—the Department of Transportation has jurisdiction (i.e., control) over the roadways in a state (Ex: TxDOT = Texas Department of Transportation).

draftsman—a person skilled in computer drafting programs and building design. Often, a draftsman position is filled by an architectural intern or interior design intern working toward licensure.

easement—restriction on a piece of property allowing others to use and access the property. An easement may cause restrictions for the church's potential use of the property.

energy codes—minimum requirements for energy efficiency in building design and construction.

engineers—a professional engineer, or "P.E." Note: a "field engineer," which is a common position on a construction team, is typically not a licensed individual, and refers to a different position.

feasibility study—a concentrated effort to determine whether an idea is financially, strategically, functionally, and aesthetically feasible. This study typically involves a design team working for a short time to address one or more possibilities (sometimes for land purchases and other opportunities).

F, F, & E—shorthand for Furniture, Fixtures, and Equipment.

fire safety—as related to a design and construction project, items needed by code to create safety during a fire for building users. For example: rules prohibiting dead-end corridors, requiring fire sprinkler systems in buildings of a certain size, and requiring fire extinguishers and easy access to the building for the fire department.

flood plain—an area (usually close to a body of water) which will flood when the body of water reaches capacity, or a low-lying area which is likely to flood.

fresh air requirements—a requirement by the mechanical code to introduce a certain amount of fresh air into a building.

fundraising—the gathering of voluntary donations. Online fundraising, pledges, events and strategic planning are all important parts of fundraising.

geotechnical report (or, soil test)—samples of dirt (also called "core samples") taken to determine the structural bearing capacity of the soil; that is, how much weight the dirt can sustain. The results of this test will tell you what type of foundation the building will need (slab on grade, piers, etc.).

glue laminated timber (glulam)—a structural system for building which is made up of layers of lumber bonded together with a moisture-resistant structural adhesive.

grades—the height above the ground at which an element exists. When dealing with a piece of land, grades usually indicate "height above sea level". Slopes and contours of the site are documented and designed using grades.

interview—a formal meeting where questions are asked and answers are given, typically related to hiring a company to complete a task.

impervious development—includes surfaces such as concrete where water will run off rather than soaking in naturally. For example, both a concrete sidewalk and a building are impervious surfaces when figuring detention requirements.

low-cost, low-commitment services—the concept of working with a company (here, an architect and construction partner) to complete relatively small tasks for a reasonable fee, reserving the ability to forgo additional work should the relationship not be beneficial for either party. This relationship is appropriate for services such as feasibility studies, master plans, and general programming; it is not appropriate for the design and construction of building projects.

master plan—a long-term outline for a series of projects for a church which, when completed, accomplish the appropriate facilities for growth and full ministry potential of the church. A master plan is meant to offer guidance and vision, as opposed to rigidity, to the various groups who will implement the different phases of the development.

means—resources and procedures necessary to complete a construction project.

mechanical zones—the areas in a building served by a piece of mechanical equipment or air conditioning unit (Ex: "We would like the church offices on a separate zone since they are open all week long.").

MEP Engineer—a professional engineer or engineering company who handles the mechanical, electrical and plumbing engineering portions of a design. Typically the "MEP Engineer" refers to a company, and the three disciplines are handled by different individuals working for the same company.

metal building—a structural system, composed of pre-engineered metal members (see also, **pre-engineered metal building**).

metes and bounds—a way to describe the lines created in a boundary survey. The metes and bounds refer to the distances and directions of the property lines, based on the points of reference (usually pins in the ground).

methods—the manner in which a contractor goes about getting a project done. (Ex: The architect should not comment on which type of trailer is being used because means and methods are the contractor's responsibility).

Mother's Day Out program (MDO)—related to design and construction, a Mother's Day Out program has a different **occupancy type** than a worship space and should be evaluated differently at the beginning of **programming** to determine what unique codes will apply.

occupancy type—a set of categories for buildings based on what they are used for, giving a framework to enforce fire safety regulations. A church is almost always categorized as an "A3," or an Assembly Space for Worship.

parameters—guidelines which create a reasonable area for successfully accomplishing work (Ex: An architect might say, "We will defer to the contractor to offer some budget parameters for that part of the project.").

parking requirements—how many parking spaces you are required to provide at a commercial building; this number is usually mandated by the city jurisdiction and based on the number of seats in your sanctuary.

partner—one who shares a common goal, divides risk, and works diligently toward the success of the group.

phased plan—the concept of deciding the sequence of which sections of a master plan or project should be constructed, and in what order (Ex: "Phase One will be the sanctuary and children's spaces, and later Phase Two will be a fellowship space and kitchen.").

pier—a structural member that carries the loads of a building, creating less reliance on the soil under the future building. Piers and their properties (size, depth, and amount of concrete and steel) are usually recommended in a **soil test** and designed by the **structural engineer**.

placemaking—intentionally creating a place with benefits on multiple levels and for multiple layers of users, with the goal of increased social interaction and closeness largely due to the common appreciation of the space.

planning—the most critical phase of a church project. The planning effort should be continuously ongoing unless a church is actively involved in the design or construction phases.

Plumbing Engineer—a professional engineer who designs the plumbing portion of a project.

plumbing fixture count requirements—the number of toilets, urinals, and sinks that you are required by law to provide in a commercial building.

pre-engineered metal building (PEMB)—a structural system composed of pre-engineered metal members.

Professional Engineer (P.E.)— an engineer who is licensed to provide design services for their area of specialty. These individuals are required by law, as are architects, on commercial projects.

programming—the process of determining how much square footage is needed in order to meet a church's needs for worship and ministry, in addition to codes and functionality.

Project Architect—a licensed architect typically responsible for the aesthetic, functional, and technical design of a building or project.

project cost—the building cost plus the soft costs, F, F & E, and design fees of a project.

Project Manager—an individual on the construction team, architectural team, or both, charged with managing the progress of the project, documentation, and the other members of the team.

quality—as related to the Budget-Scope-Quality triangular equation, quality indicates the level of detail, materials used, and manner in which specific elements are designed and constructed.

Registered Accessibility Consultant (RAS)—a person licensed by a state to review project plans and inspect completed projects with regards to accessibility.

rebar—reinforcing steel, most often used in construction for foundations or other concrete load-bearing members such as walls.

safety plan—a contractor's plan for keeping your jobsite safe. This plan should include their safety rules and training procedures.

Safety record—an account of a contractor's performance during inspections by OSHA.

schematic design (SD)—the first period of the design phase. During this phase, the goal is to reach consensus on the way a building looks. For instance, agreement would need to be reached regarding a basic site and floor plan layout and the massing and materials for the building (also referred to as "concept design").

scope—as related to the Budget-Scope-Quality triangular equation, scope indicates the amount of building and paving being designed (typically discussed in terms of square footage).

select fill—fill dirt with good structural integrity. Soil that does not expand and contract easily and provides a good substrate for a **slab on grade** or other structural system.

slab on grade—a horizontal pouring of concrete, poured directly over a prepared area of earth (the pad). The size of **rebar** and depth of beams for a slab on grade are usually specified in the **soil test**.

soil test—samples of dirt (also called "core samples") taken to determine the structural bearing capacity of the soil; that is, how much weight the dirt can sustain. The results of this test will tell you what type of foundation the building will need (slab on grade, piers, etc.). Soil tests may also be referred to as "geotechnical" or "geotech" reports.

strategic planning—an activity by a group to set priorities, confirm availability of resources and funds, and align all partners toward the same desired outcome.

structural—Any element related to the building's ability to stand up to and carry loads (wind loads, roof loads, etc.).

structural inspection—a physical inspection confirming the structural integrity or deficiency of a building. The inspection is performed by a structural engineer and includes a written report.

structural slab—a type of foundation recommended when soil conditions indicate that the soil cannot bear the load of a building due to shifting or major expanding and contracting of the soil. A structural slab is designed to create a system of voids in the foundation, using carton forms which, as part of the system (including concrete and steel), will carry the loads of a building adequately and safely.

Structural Engineer—a professional engineer who designs the structural portion of a project including the foundation and any structural systems involved.

structural steel—steel which is categorized for use as a construction material. A structural steel member's shape is intentionally specified or designed according to its properties for stiffness or ability to withstand certain loads.

substantial completion—the stage of construction when the work is sufficiently complete and ready for the church to move into the building [according to a standard AIA (American Institute of Architects) contract].

survey—a general term to describe the documentation of a property's general elements. See **topographical survey**, **boundary survey**, and **metes and bounds**.

third place—a physical place other than a person's home or work which becomes a significant part of their life for a period of time.

three-dimensional model (3D model)—a representation of a design developed using software which documents the three-dimensional properties of a space. These can be used to figure out a design and to create renderings or animations for fundraising purposes.

topographical survey (topo survey)—a survey which locates natural and man-made elements in addition to the **metes and bounds** of a property. The elevations of the land surface are documented and usually shown in a CAD-type file (these files are created on computer-aided drafting programs for building and site design). Utility lines, buildings, poles, and sidewalks will usually be shown in the topo survey.

trusses—a structural member capable of transferring a load to another structural member, usually spanning a distance (Ex: a roof truss accepts the load of the roof and transfers that load to the columns it sits on).

value engineering (VE)—a method to preserve the functionality (referred to as "value") of a design while cutting the cost (Ex: "The contractor's team offered carpet instead of tile as a VE option.").

variance—a requested deviation from a city's typical code understanding/enforcement (Ex: "The movie theater requested a variance at the council hearing because they wanted to install a much larger than average pole sign.").

vet or vetting—checking out a property in an intentional way, with consideration for your own potential use of the site.

water detention—see "**detention**."

wayfinding—the act of finding your way around through a building, campus, or space.

wood-framed building—a building which has a structural system made up of load-bearing wood members.

xeriscaping—landscaping that reduces or eliminates the need for regular watering.

INDEX

A

acoustician 74, 141
ADA 62, 102, 141
asbestos 58, 59, 125, 141

B

boundary survey 47, 142, 147, 150
brownfield sites 50, 142
building cost 36, 99, 106, 125, 130, 142, 148
building performance 100, 142
building permit 53, 54, 59, 99, 125, 143

C

civil engineer 48, 49, 51, 52, 116, 122, 143
commercial building 96, 97, 118, 143, 147, 148
construction documents 123, 142, 143, 144
construction phase 105, 110, 111, 118, 131, 143, 148
construction team 57, 119, 143, 144, 148
contaminants 50, 143
culture 10, 11, 21, 22, 40, 42, 43, 61, 63, 66, 85, 86, 87, 88, 107, 126, 136, 137

D

detention 51, 52, 54, 55, 64, 65, 90, 96, 143, 144, 146, 151
draftsman 116, 121, 144

E

energy codes 100, 144

F

feasibility study 35, 44, 45, 58, 61, 64, 65, 145

G

grades 47, 145

YOUR

STRATEGIC RESOURCES TO
ORGANIZE YOUR CHURCH VISION

Start your planning today with all the tools you need:

- Easy-to-use spreadsheets

- Guided tools to articulate your vision for growth

- Checklists to get you organized

Plan ahead so that you can grow with confidence!

www.churchbuildingguide.com

www.ingramcontent.com/pod-product-compliance
Lightning Source LLC
Chambersburg PA
CBHW050507210326
41521CB00011B/2361